*W*HITE *C*RANE *W*ISDOM *S*ERIES

White Crane Institute's guiding principle: "fostering the gathering and dissemination of information about the critical role sexuality and gender has played and continues to play in the development of cultural, spiritual and religious traditions and to provide a nurturing environment for the continuation and expansion of those explorations for the greater good of all society."

As Gay people we bear wisdom. As Gay people we create culture. White Crane is proud to present these valuable treasures through our Gay Wisdom Series. Our aim is to provide you with fine books of insight, discernment and spiritual discovery.

ALL

A James Broughton Reader

Edited by Jack Foley

White Crane
Books

editor@gaywisdom.org
www.gaywisdom.org

Cover art copyright © 2006 by Sou MacMillan
Photo by Joel Singer
Interior book design by Toby Johnson

Published as a trade paperback original, 2006
by White Crane Books, 172 Fifth Avenue, Suite 69, Brooklyn NY 11217
Re-released by White Crane Books, 2013

ISBN-13 978-1-938246-05-0
ISBN-10 1-938246-05-5

White Crane Institute is a 501(c)(3) education corporation, committed to the certainty that gay consciousness plays a special and important role in the evolution of life on Earth. White Crane Institute publishes White Crane, the Journal of Gay Wisdom & Culture. Your contributions and support are tax-deductible to the fullest extent of the law. White Crane Institute, 172 Fifth Avenue, Suite 69, Brooklyn NY 11217.

Allness is ripe.

James Broughton
1913-1999

Preface

White Crane Institute is proud to make the writings of poet and filmmaker James Broughton available again; some of the material in this book have never before been published.

Certainly to have a new collection of James Broughton's work that renders the arch of his magical life is a reason enough to celebrate. But in our on-going efforts to make significant gay culture and spiritual thinking available more widely, there is a distinction that can and should be made between those who were (and are) "gay artists" and those who made art "gaily."

James is, quintessentially, the latter. Nowhere is the sheer effervescence of gayness more clearly demonstrated than in the lifework and writings of James Broughton. Nowhere is joy of life proclaimed with more fervor and an almost divine obliviousness to any form of shame. The depth and mythology of gay love has never been more innocently and vociferously celebrated; the proud reclaiming of "queer" can, arguably, be traced to Broughton. No one has explored the full dimensions of a vibrant eros more deliciously than he did with every word he wrote, every frame he shot… with every moment of his life. If poetry is the language of the soul, Broughton had an unparalleled fluency. If film is one of the truly American contributions to world culture, Broughton was its gay ambassador. And, as always he said it best:

"To assert, to assert. To mate Eros to Logos. To sing the divine unions!"

White Crane Institute is grateful to the artist Joel Singer, James Broughton's loving partner for the most creative years of his life, for

8

bringing this manuscript to our door and for the loving portrait of James that graces the cover.

We want to thank San Francisco poet and KPFA radio host, Jack Foley for his thoughtful and loving notes and guidance through the sparkling mind that was James Broughton and the additional time he gave to us to assist us in putting this in the hands of readers and making sure it was as polished a gem as it turned out to be.

8

Bo Young / Brooklyn
Dan Vera / Washington D.C

T*able of* C*ontents*

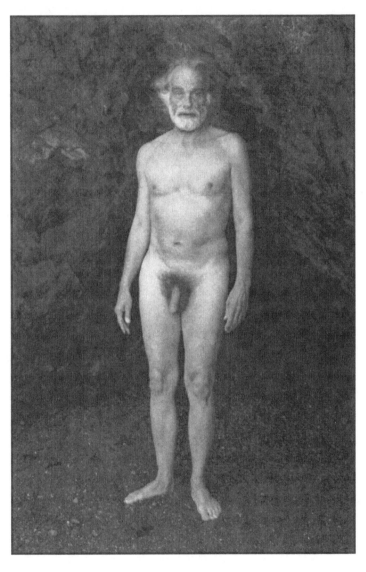

"A Long Undressing"
James Broughton on the Mendocino coast, 1976
Photo by Joel Singer

*I*ntroduction to
All: A James Broughton Reader

by Jack Foley

> Love can become a good habit, like cleaning one's teeth.
>
> — *James Broughton*

> It is the business of life to eschew introductions.
>
> — *Anonymous*

Remembering a particularly fatuous remark made by an Easterner, a defender of James Broughton's angrily remarked, "That idiot thinks Broughton is unimportant." "No," came the reply from still another defender, "he just thinks Broughton is California."

Poet/filmmaker James Broughton is California in significant ways —not least of which is his brilliantly skewed use of both film and verse. "Don't waste your time making a film like anyone else's," he advises in *Making Light of It:*

> That's duplication of effort. Besides, it won't be any good. Your business is to make something that neither you nor I have ever seen before. Your business is to make a wonderful new kind of mess in your own way.

This *James Broughton Reader* is an attempt to express the importance of James Broughton not only as a California writer but as an American writer. It is meant as a companion volume to Broughton's most recent selected poetry, *Packing Up for Paradise: Selected Poems 1946-1996* (Black Sparrow Press, 1997). The fact that James Broughton—who considered himself essentially a poet—expressed himself in many media and that his sexuality was as shape-shifting as his free-flowing imagination makes him not less but more American. Imagine Thoreau with an obstreperous, widely-responsive body and a wicked sense of humor; and then imagine him a world traveler, a particularly individualistic Jungian and Zen Buddhist—and a filmmaker.

In a lifetime that stretched from 1913 to 1999, James Broughton witnessed and commented on most of the twentieth century. His commentary was leveled at some of the century's most precious myths, but it was never made from the point of view of officialdom; rather, from the point of view of the outsider. The commentary was, however, never of the "rationalist" variety. Broughton was no deconstructionist; he countered myth with myth. In a century struggling with religious belief, he asserted a religion of "Big Joy." In a century whose central art form was film, he made movies—"alternative" ones. In a century struggling to find a place and definition for "outsider" groups such as gays and women, he became an emblem of that struggle, though he also married and experienced the life of a more or less conventional husband and father. In a century aghast at its own horrors, he advocated laughter. His name for his outsider status was "poet," and, as he knew very well, poetry was one of the century's most innovative but least mainstream forms. Yet—unlike most poetic innovators of the century—he was never a poet of the ivory tower variety. Despite his advocacy of deep ecology and of the notion of the earth as "mother," Broughton remained a deeply urban figure, an essentially communal outsider who simultaneously believed and was amused by the notion that an active poet could change the world. In the midst of an immensely rationalist and unbelieving century, which longed intensely for some sort of transcendental assurance, he asserted mystery. Though he occasionally thought of himself as God, he never took himself (or God) quite seriously.

*

There's a story James Broughton told over and over again in various works, a primal experience that determined his life. Its fullest manifestation was in his memoir, *Coming Unbuttoned* (1993). "One night when I was three years old," he writes, "I was awakened by a glittering stranger who told me I was a poet and always would be and never to fear being alone or being laughed at. That was my first meeting with my angel, who is the most interesting poet I have ever met":

> *It must have happened on an autumn night of 1916 before my brother was born. I remember waking in the dark and hearing my parents arguing in the next room. But a more persistent sound, a kind of whirring whistle, spun a light across the ceiling. I stood up in my crib and looked into the backyard. Over the neighbor's palm tree a pulsing headlamp came whistling directly toward me. When it had whirled right up to my window, out of its radiance stepped a naked boy. He was at least three years older than I but he looked all ages at once. He had no wings, but I knew he was angel-sent: his laughing beauty illuminated the night and his melodious voice enraptured my ears.*
>
> *I didn't know what his words meant but I understood everything he said. And he said a lot. He said I could call him Hermy though that was not his real name. He knew my name because it was on his agenda. He represented a company whose business was health care for the soul. And he wanted me to work for them.*

Hermy has an important message for the little boy: "He insisted I would always be a poet even if I tried not to be":

> *As he spoke he drew forth from the glow between his legs a pulsing hot sparkler, which laughed the way he did. Raising it like a wand he circled my head with stars, then spilled them on my brow, my throat, my chest, all the way down to my peepee. The hot sparks made me giggle. When he blessed me that way I knew I would always belong to him...*
>
> *Suddenly Hermy blew out his throbbing wand, spun back into his searchlight and zoomed out of sight over the palm tree just as I*

heard my mother enter from her bedroom: "Good Lord, baby! Why
are you standing up? Are you sick? Heavens, you've wet your
jammies again!"

The encounter with Hermy/Hermes is one of those stories
Broughton describes as "true" even if it never happened. It is his myth
of origin, his "roots," and the issues it raises—issues of imagination,
sexuality, childhood, magic, initiation, transformation—echo throughout
his life. Every element of the story is important, but perhaps its most
important aspect is the fact that it happens in the dark and that it
involves the little boy seeing something. Little James, the three-year-old
poet/filmmaker-to-be, is having an ecstatic experience of the hermetic
art of cinema. He is watching a movie, and it is a movie that is being
played for himself alone. It is not a mass-produced film; it is special and
private and initiatory. It is not for everyone, but for the person who can
receive it, it will change his life. The films and poetry Broughton went on
to make, varied as they are, are all versions of this primary experience,
this ur-movie. They all involve magic, nakedness (metaphorical as well
as literal) and growth. Like Hermy's appearance, they are full, frontal
attacks, which contain an element of danger. They want to give us a
powerful, sexual experience of the wonder of this world. They want
to make us wet our jammies.

The Life

A third generation Californian, James Richard Broughton was born
in the valley town of Modesto in 1913. Though he traveled and later
lived in Washington state, he grew up in San Francisco and spent most of
his life in or near that city. What he later called "the Great Unconscious
of the Pacific Ocean" figures prominently in his work. As a young man,
he attended Stanford University, where he encountered Yvor Winters,
but left before finishing his B.A. degree—and with a decidedly low
opinion of Winters. His first film, *Mother's Day* (1948), was edited in
his bedroom and prophetically hailed by his friend the late Ruth Witt-
Diamant (founder, in 1953, of the San Francisco Poetry Center) as "the
most important work since Pavlov's dog."

Broughton's first published book was *The Playground* (Centaur
Press, 1949), a verse play, which bears some resemblance to *Mother's*

Day. (*Mother's Day* was initially conceived of as a film version of *The Playground.*) His second book was *Musical Chairs* (1950). His literary work began to appear in various venues, notably in Donald Allen's landmark 1960 anthology, *The New American Poetry* as well as in the famous "San Francisco Scene" issue of *The Evergreen Review* (1957), where he can be found alongside the likes of Allen Ginsberg ("Howl," bowdlerized, appeared in that issue), Jack Kerouac, Lawrence Ferlinghetti, Henry Miller, Robert Duncan, and Michael McClure.

When *Mother's Day* appeared, Broughton was not a very young man. He was 35 years old. His father had died in an influenza epidemic when the poet was a child, and his mother had died of cancer in 1939, two days before her fiftieth birthday. Childhood was long behind him—a fact that is expressed in the film by having adults play the children. Nor was the poet at this point very close to the "Sunny Jim" he had been called as a baby. "When I was 30," he wrote, "my greatest consolation was the thought of suicide." And again: "Cinema saved me from suicide when I was 32 by revealing to me a wondrous reality: the love between fellow artists."

Mother's Day begins with a family photograph album, but one of its major points is that a film is not a photograph album: it is a film. "Mother," the central figure of these "indelible memories" of the director's San Francisco childhood, is the "indifferent goddess disapproving of romp and spoof"; she is not only a deadening influence on everything around her—a sort of failed Medusa—but also a bastion of the old technology. Mother is associated with the static world of tintypes; she attempts to keep everything (Mother's word) "lovely"—and under wraps.

It becomes clear that Mother's deepest fault is her attempt to turn people into photographs—into material for her scrapbook. But the children don't want to be "stills," they want to be characters in a film. They want to "play" and in particular, they want to move. For Broughton film has little to do with painting or still photography, but it has a great deal to do with dance. "Film direction," he will state, "is closer to choreography than to Stanislavsky … film is a new kind of ballet … and its subject matter [is] the whole dance of life." Mother, it seems, is everything that films are not; she is making an active effort not to "dance."

If we examine the themes of Broughton's early work—*Mother's Day* (1948), the verse drama, *The Playground* (1949), the poems in *Musical Chairs* (1950)—we will hardly find it surprising that the artist at thirty-something had thoughts of suicide. The world these works explore is brilliant and hilarious, but it is also profoundly disturbing, even, at times, terrifying. *The Playground* is subtitled "A Play for Precarious Grown-ups." *Musical Chairs* is subtitled "Songs for Anxious Children." Discussing *Mother's Day* Broughton asked, "Do we remember that children are often incomprehensibly terror-stricken, are always ready to slip over into some private nonsense-ritual, or into behavior based upon their misconception of the adult world?" The world of these early works is one of incomprehensible terror, of anxiety, of "some private nonsense-ritual." It is a world in which a "playground" tends inexplicably to become a "mausoleum," in which "childhood" is barely distinguishable from "dying."

Mother's Day, The Playground and *Musical Chairs* were all written when Broughton was about thirty-five, the age at which the Jungian process of "individuation" is said to begin. These works may well have been the mode by which the poet experienced that process. (Jungian themes return repeatedly in both his films and his poetry.) In any case, these early works allowed him to come suddenly face to face with everything his childhood meant to him—and what it meant was, precisely, death:

> To have been lanced,
> the blade run through the very center,
> to be beginning to grow rot:
> when what I sought (or thought)
> was a beginning to go running
> with flowing blade and pennant for the sunlight
> dance
> ("At the Sword Race")

Yet in saying this I am speaking only of Broughton's content, only of what the works, or some parts of the works, are "saying." The form of the work—with its dizzying variety of modes, its wit, its dazzling shifts between the "adult" and the "childish"—is anything but "struggling" or "stalled": it is energetic, bold, innovative—alive.

In effect, the work's form is an energetic and creative response to the sense of death, which its content nevertheless manifests everywhere. Broughton's discovery of the "energy" of film, of the fact that films, unlike "the portrait photograph," MOVE, was also a discovery of the "energy" of life. Film—whose "subject matter," he says, "is the whole dance of life"—appeared to him to be an embodiment of the very energy he was seeking:

> A little arson, please, a little aerification
> to dare some miracle of small surprises!
> At least a bauble, at least!
> Or so are we stalled, in our labyrinths.
> ("Call for a Desperate Measure")

Broughton is fascinated by the exact moment at which motion— which is to say, life—emerges out of stillness, the moment at which the "photograph" is suddenly and magically transformed into the "film." This magical moment, presided over by the god Hermes, is also the moment at which "mere prose" metamorphoses into poetry. Broughton spent his life attempting to "catch" that moment in one way or another:

> Only when I glee
> am I me.
> ("Only When I")

Yet "death" in Broughton is never something one faces and conquers once and for all. It is something that remains at the edge of consciousness and can at times assert itself in full force. The sense of the presence of death returned to Broughton in a different form when the poet turned sixty:

> *When on my sixtieth birthday in 1973 I was honored with retrospective exhibits in London and in New York, I felt it was time to fold up my career as a filmmaker. I had produced seven films in ten years. I thought I had said everything I had to say, except perhaps for some graceful farewell. Besides, my sagging energies were reflected in my home life. In the marriage bed I had encountered the consternation*

of impotence.

"Had my soul tottered off to sleep / taking my potency with it?" he asks in "Wondrous the Merge" (*Ecstasies*, 1983):

> Had they both retired before I could
> leaving me a classroom somnambulist?
> Why else should I at sixty-one
> feel myself shriveling into fadeout?

Discussing the process of "Individuation," Jungian psychotherapist Marie-Louise von Franz asserts in *Man and His Symbols* that "the character of a man's anima"—the "feminine" side of a man's unconscious—"is as a rule shaped by his mother":

> *If he feels that his mother had a negative influence on him, his anima will often express itself in irritable, depressed moods, uncertainty, insecurity, and touchiness. (If, however, he is able to overcome the negative assaults on himself, they can serve to reinforce his masculinity.) Within the soul of such a man the negative mother-anima figure will endlessly repeat this theme: "I am nothing. Nothing makes any sense. With others it's different, but for me … I enjoy nothing." These "anima moods" cause a sort of dullness, a fear of disease, of impotence, or of accidents. The whole of life takes on a sad and oppressive aspect. Such dark moods can even lure a man to suicide, in which case the anima becomes a death demon.*

In Broughton's moment of need, Hermy appeared again in the person of a twenty-five-year-old Canadian film student named Joel Singer:

> Then on a cold seminar Monday
> in walked an unannounced redeemer
> disguised as a taciturn student
> Brisk and resolute in scruffy mufti
> he set down his backpack shook his hair
> and offered me unequivocal devotion
>
> He dismissed my rebuffs and ultimatums

He scoffed at suggestions of disaster
He insisted he had been given authority
to provide my future happiness
Was it possible he had been sent
from some utopian headquarters?

Broughton's meeting with Singer was a life-changing, life-determining moment that animated his consciousness with a power that lasted until his death. He and Singer were married on Christmas Eve, 1976. "Joel brought me true 'psychic wholeness' by giving me the missing reality of myself," Broughton wrote in *Coming Unbuttoned*. "At last I could become fully my own kind of man, giving in as well as cutting loose. Reinvigorated I was ready to begin life anew." In his later work—with Singer as muse, companion, lover, dearest friend—Broughton becomes not only a poet but a shaman, an artist acutely aware of his role as a worker in the world of art and in the gay community.

*

Who exactly is "James Broughton"? One answer is: He is the man who made all those films and wrote all those books. If one deals with a personality as mercurial and protean as Broughton's, it is not possible to arrive at any "final" summary. The works speak for themselves and for a great many other things as well. In all of them, boundaries are continually asserted and then dissolved—boundaries between self and other, between male and female.

Many of us feel that our bodies are boundaries, insisting through their fascinating but demanding "parts" that we belong irrevocably to one sex or to the other. And yet: do we? Bodies are a subject of Broughton's intense cinematic scrutiny. But his—position—is hardly a monolithic one. "Always I had wondered," he writes in *The Androgyne Journal*, "why men retain vestigial nipples. Now I no longer question. They are not vestigial, they are the living doors to the chamber of the Goddess. She is present in every man's breast. She lives in every man's womb." In Broughton it is precisely the experience of the body that allows us to discover that the body's supposed limitations are not limitations at all. Again from *The Androgyne Journal*: "I have but to stroke my nipples tenderly and at once she responds to my caress. She wakens the He in me. My penis asserts a thrust like the roaring heat of the Alchemical Lion. Inexplicable magic!"

In all his works James Broughton is a poet who deliberately stays attentive to whatever "scattered remains"—to use the title of his last film—he can find; who deliberately honors the complicated, even at times contradictory richness of his nature:

> Can you accept yourself, in every part and particular? Specifically, tenderly and humbly? Can you learn to love yourself with gusto?... Will I ever accept that I am many men and many women trying to live together?

> (The Androgyne Journal)

Appropriately, Making Light of It, the filmmaker's book on the art of film, concludes with a passage that sends us back to that moment when, standing erect in his crib before a whirling "radiance," young James discovered his vocation:

> One must always do the impossible. Art itself is impossible. Trust the passion, the way of seeing, the zest of creating. There is no meaningful life without poetry and nothing is art that lacks it.

> What unimagined radiance will yet emerge from the flickering dark?

*

On Wednesday, May 19, 1999, Joel Singer phoned to tell me that James had died peacefully on Monday of that week at the age of eighty-five. In an interview appearing in Poetry Flash (Number 280, February 1999), Broughton says, "Of course we miss people. You can indulge your grief. But if you care about them you want to wish them Godspeed. Into the arms of God":

> Suffering can't be avoided. I think the way to happiness is to go into the darkness of yourself. That's the place the seed is nourished, takes its roots and grows up, and becomes ultimately the plant and the flower. You can only go upward by first going downward. I've

never been afraid of losing my beautiful neurosis as a source of my poetry. [Laughter.]

What I've tried to present in this Reader is both a sampling of Broughton's work and the outline, the arc of a life.

A Note on the Structure of
All: A James Broughton Reader

The three short pieces that open the book—"On the Androgyne," "I Am in Love with All Things Erect," and "I Have the God"—are brief suggestions of themes that remain with Broughton throughout his life. The pieces deal with sexuality, creativity, the play of opposites, mystical religious feelings, (homo)eroticism and, most of all, with the "Androgyne," which is Broughton's figure for the whole of his consciousness—and for wholeness itself.

These pieces are followed by selections from *Coming Unbuttoned*, Broughton's autobiography. Though Broughton's consciousness ranged widely, it remained rooted in the events of his life, so that some understanding of the life is necessary if we are to understand the work. These selections from the autobiography deal with the poet's childhood and are followed by the complete verse play, *The Playground*, Broughton's first published book. No longer in print, *The Playground* is a fascinating presentation of the poet's early view of the world, his initial thrust towards understanding. Taken together, the autobiography and *The Playground* evoke a childhood, which in many ways determines the whole of Broughton's life.

These works are followed by *The Androgyne Journal*, a brilliant book of self-discovery in which Broughton discovers a new way of dealing with the Death Mother that has plagued him since childhood: here he imagines a mythological creature, the Androgyne, that embodies life in its fullness. The Androgyne is at once Broughton himself and the god—his god—Hermes. The Androgyne's bodily ecstasy—both physical and metaphysical—is a dynamic answer to the presence of the Death Mother. But the Death Mother is not the final form death takes. In Broughton's late poems—some of the finest poems of old age anyone has written—death becomes a lover, the Androgyne himself: "It is rumored that Jesus is in the neighborhood / looking for some body to resurrect."

For many people, James Broughton is primarily a filmmaker. The imaginative high point represented by *The Androgyne Journal* is followed by two sections dealing with Broughton on film, a medium which was never separate in his mind from poetry, sexuality, etc. For Broughton, cinema—like everything he considered—is constantly mythologized. His descriptions of the films are of value because they suggest themes Broughton was dealing with as he actually made the films—even though the finished films sometimes differ from the descriptions—and because they shed considerable light on all of his work.

No collection of James Broughton's writing would be complete without a presentation of his highly individualistic version of Zen Buddhism. These delightful works mingle seriousness with "superior wackiness" and reflect the period of Broughton's life when he was most influenced by his friend Alan Watts.

These poems are followed by a wonderful, never-before-published travel journal Broughton wrote in 1979. In it he deals with his commitment to Joel Singer, whom he had married in 1976, and to the gay world in general. His "three week honeymoony voyage"—and his separation from his wife Suzanna—brings him to still another aspect of the Androgyne. He is giddy with his new-found freedom:

> He caresses my soul
> He explodes my soul
> I am rolling in ecstasy with his blessing

If Broughton can ever be said to be "sober," he becomes so in the next section, "Shaman Psalm / Erogeny," in which the Androgyne takes on not only a private but a public meaning: Broughton's relationship with Singer is now understood not only as something of interest to Broughton personally but of a more general interest. Singer's love represents an extraordinary number of things to Broughton, but one of them is definitely a gateway to the divine: "God is my Beloved /

God and I are lovers." This relationship—the experience of Godhood through the ecstasies of a human lover—is one, Broughton firmly believes, that can be experienced by all men. His work thus becomes a celebration of such possibility: "Listen Brothers Listen... This is the hour for / amorous revolt."

As James Broughton grew older, he wrote some extraordinarily fine poems and comments about old age—a subject which English/ American literature has somewhat slighted. *"Old Scorpio: Poems of Old Age"* presents some of these considerations of "creeping decrepitude." This section is followed by an interview I did in which the poet eloquently reflects upon the progress and meaning of his whole life. The interview was conducted on the day before Broughton's eighty-fourth birthday. The book closes with Broughton's joyful hymn to life, "Behold the Bridegrooms: A connubial masque for James and Joel." The masque ends with a "general dance"—Broughton frequently referred to "the whole dance of life"—and the words "Aaahhh! Aaahhh! Aaahhh! / Bliss! Bliss! Bliss!" The little afterword, wittily titled "Song of Song,"suggests that all the turns and permutations of James Broughton's consciousness were nothing but "the song you have been singing / all your life." This book is both a presentation and an echo of that song. As a "reader," it is the very first book to allow the various aspects of Broughton's complex personality to "sing" to one another.

On The Androgyne

Among mystics of the early church a new type of humanity was expected to emerge when a fusion of the sexes produced a new unpolarized consciousness.

The power inherent in both sexes, when brought together, create a great symbol of dynamic unity.

Both St. Paul and St. John considered androgyny one of the characteristics of spiritual perfection.

Hesiod claimed that bisexuality is one of the glories of divinity.

Life becomes a search for the Inner Unity that the Divine Androgyne symbolizes.

Your birthright was double-sexed: half from the mother, half from the father.

Philosophically speaking one cannot be anything par excellence unless one is at the same time its opposite.

I am in love with all things erect

I am in love with the erections of man
steeples derricks pyramids
pillars and pylons towers and turrets
totem poles flagpoles pole vaults

I am in love with things firmly erected
minarets pagodas campaniles
all the monumentalities of man

I am in love with all things erect
particularly homo sapiens erectus
the tower that lies down and can arise again

man the phenomenal erection

I have the god

I have the god in my mouth

I savor the taste on my tongue
the sweet taste with the bitter

I have the god in my mouth

I relish the nip of desire
the peppery succulence

I have the god in my mouth

I sip the flavors of zest
the tang of gusto and punch

I have the god in my mouth

I feast on the spicy glory
devour the holy delicious

I swallow the god in my mouth

I sanctify in my throat
am sanctified into my guts

I have the god   I have the god
I have the god in my mouth

FROM COMING UNBUTTONED

These selections from Broughton's memoir are taken from the opening two chapters, "Into This World and Out of It" and "Dormitory Initiations."

*T*he year that gave birth to *Le Sacre du Printemps, Swann's Way,* and *Nude Descending a Staircase* also brought me into this world. Those other blessed events of 1913 required a more laborious parturition than I did. Dr. Robertson declared mine the happiest delivery he had ever attended. For one thing I sailed in easy and laughing. And because I smiled at everyone they called me Sunny Jim. This happened in the town of Modesto on the Tuolumne River of Stanislaus County in the state of California.

My mother once confessed that giving birth to me was the orgasmic highlight of her life. In fact, she and I got along better in her womb than we ever did after I came out of it. She adored babies but disliked children, disliked indeed any person who ignored her instructions. Once I crawled around on my own she found plenty to dislike.

My initial misdemeanor remained the most unforgivable. No firstborn son of hers had any right turning out to be a poet. She had planned it: I was to be a surgeon, marry a girl from a good family, play golf with Republicans, and earn uncountable sums of money. After all, my grandfathers were bankers, and so was my father. Poets didn't know how to earn money and didn't care to know. They led disreputable lives and died young. Besides, most of them were sissies and everyone knew that sissies wouldn't defend themselves, wouldn't even fight for their country. They went on the stage or got arrested for indecent behavior. If Sunny Jim showed such tendencies she would have to squelch them at once. Thus, although I was born cheerful, my mother did her utmost to beat the cheer out of me.

Named Olga Matilda Jungbluth, my mother held stern Prussian notions of how a man should act. Her grandfather embodied this ideal of manhood. Nicholas Ohlandt had arrived from Germany with only seven dollars in his pocket (so went the family legend) and when he departed for Cypress Lawn Cemetery he was president of the San Francisco Bank where he made money and president of the National Ice Company where he made ice cream. Olga was his favorite in the family and she adored him in return. She named my baby brother Nicholas in the hope that he would grow into a great tycoon. Though he was not a sissy, he too proved to be an economic disappointment.

Olga had little patience with my father's diffidence toward moneymaking. She also deplored his small-town heritage. Orphaned as a child, she had been raised in a lap of luxury by the Ohlandts in their Queen Anne mansion on a San Francisco hilltop. To have ended her honeymoon in a dinky bungalow in a flat farming town of the San Joaquin Valley was both an indignity and a tribulation. In this bungalow—1015 16th Street, Modesto, California—Dr. Robertson introduced me to planet Earth when the sun was in Scorpio, the moon in Aires, and Libra rising. My mother was a double Virgo.

Three years later in this same bungalow I experienced the major epiphany of my life. In a book and a film I have described the experience thus: "One night when I was three years old I was awakened by a glittering stranger who told me I was a poet and always would be and never to fear being alone or being laughed at. That was my first meeting with my angel, who is the most interesting poet I have ever met.

The actual event was not so concisely perceived. Being so much a part of everything he sees, a wide-eyed child is an imprecise reporter. Nor does my statement of the fact mean that anyone has believed it. In 1942 a psychiatrist in West Los Angeles scoffed at me: "That shows how weak your sense of reality has always been." William Blake would have believed me. But then Blake never went to a therapist. He knew that poets never lie, they merely embroider.

It must have happened on an autumn night of 1916 before my brother was born. I remember waking in the dark and hearing my parents arguing in the next room. But a more persistent sound, a kind of whirring whistle, spun a light across the ceiling. I stood up in my crib and looked into the backyard. Over the neighbor's palm tree a pulsing headlamp came whistling directly toward me. When it had whirled right up to my window, out of its radiance stepped a naked boy. He was at least three years older than I but he looked all ages at once. He had no wings, but I knew he was angel-sent: his laughing beauty illuminated the night and his melodious voice enraptured my ears.

I didn't know what his words meant but I understood everything he said. And he said a lot. He said I could call him Hermy though that was not his real name. He knew my name because it was on his agenda. He represented a company whose business was health care for the soul. And he wanted me to work for them.

He insisted I would always be a poet even if I tried not to be. He offered me three gifts that he said would come in handy: intuition, articulation, and merriment. Poets, he explained, believe in the unbelievable, worship wonder, celebrate life. Despite what I might hear to the contrary the world was not a miserable prison, it was a playground for a nonstop tournament between stupidity and imagination. If I followed the game sharply enough I could be a useful spokesman for Big Joy. I know this is what he said because he told me the same sort of thing at many a later meeting.

As he spoke he drew forth from the glow between his legs a pulsing hot sparkler, which laughed the way he did. Raising it like a wand he circled my head with stars, then spilled them on my brow, my throat, my chest, all the way down to my peepee. The hot sparks made me giggle.

When he blessed me that way I knew I would always belong to him. (I realize now that he neglected to bless my feet. Perhaps angels don't think much about feet. This may account for my difficulty in standing my ground as well as my tendency to collapse upwards.)

Suddenly Hermy blew out his throbbing wand, spun back into his searchlight and zoomed out of sight over the palm tree just as I heard my mother enter from her bedroom: "Good Lord, baby! Why are you standing up? Are you sick? Heavens, you've wet your jammies again!"

I never told my mother about my secret visitor. She had short patience with extraterrestrial mysteries. Marrying into an Episcopalian family had only increased her irritation with the inexplicable. Moral prejudices were sufficient for her. When it came to dealing with sin she venerated surgeons because they could cut the bad out of one. I had to keep many secrets from her for fear she would have me operated on regularly. All my life Hermy remained my biggest secret.

I would like to have told my father. He seemed pleased that I was growing up. But I had too little chance to share his company. He died two years later.

At an art auction in 1959 a hostess pouring me a cup of tea remarked: "Your father was the handsomest man I ever met in my entire life." She had been his classmate at Berkeley in 1904. "Irwin Broughton was a real knockout," she added. On the other hand my mother, who never attended university, had this to say: "Your father drove me crazy. I never had any idea what he was thinking."

For me he was never less than a godlike figure with his warm bulk, his arms that lifted me aloft, his resonant voice. I especially remember rides with him: riding on his shoulders at a Fourth of July parade, riding in the saddle with him on one of Bob McHenry's palominos at the Bald Eagle Ranch, riding down a slide in a wooden boat at an amusement park. He never made fun of me. He didn't seem to worry that I preferred Raggedy Andy to a baseball bat. My behavior amused more than annoyed him. Like the occasion in the Santa Cruz mountains during the last summer of his life when, dressed up for dinner at the resort hotel, I fell into Boulder Creek. I had leaned too far over the water reaching for a frog. When Irwin pulled me out dripping and crying he consoled me warmly whereas Olga berated me for ruining my brand-new sailor suit.

The most disturbing memory I have of my father happened the night Olga ordered him to punish me. After my brother's birth we had moved from Modesto to a house on Clay Street in San Francisco near my mother's relatives. My father worked in the Federal Reserve. One day, after slapping me several times, Olga fumed, "I'm tired of trying to discipline you. When your father comes home I'll get him to give you a good beating. Maybe he can teach you not to be so naughty."

When I heard Irwin enter the house I hid in the hall closet behind the carpet sweeper. Olga told him that I had gone the limit this time: 'Do you know what that little devil did? He put on my new feathered turban and then emptied a bottle of Milk of Magnesia over Baby Nick. The rug is ruined."

I squinched as far into the corner as I could. When he pulled me out I felt more fearful than guilty. Whereas Olga frequently swatted me as though I were a bothersome fly, Irwin had never raised his hand to me. Now pushing me along the back hall he announced, "I'm taking you down to the basement, young man, to teach you a lesson."

We descended the steep stairs into the cellar, which housed the furnace and the water heater and the lawn mower. But once there Irwin stopped and stood still. He didn't start to whip me, he seemed to forget all about me. When he did recollect why we were there, he sighed, "You shouldn't upset your mother so much, she's high-strung."

Gently he took me by the hand and sat me down beside him on the bottom stair. Then he put his arm around my shoulder and drew me close to him. For the longest time he held me in his arms, emitting occasional gasps and weary sighs. He stared into the dark as he spoke:

"Do you remember Justin? My friend Justin? When he was last here we took you to Idora Park, do you remember, and we rode on the Chute-the-Chutes?"

I not only remembered how the boat slid down into a splashing lake, I remember sitting between my father and a red-bearded fellow who shouted "Ship Ahoy!" Never before had I seen my father so boisterous. But here in the cold basement his body slumped heavily upon me as he murmured, "He's gone. Justin's gone—he's gone for good." And he began to cry.

Years later I learned that on the very day of his not spanking me Irwin had received news of his friend's death in a French hospital. Justin had been fatally wounded in the Battle of the Marne.

When I was in my teens my father's sister told me how much Justin meant to Irwin, how they had been close chums in college, had trekked in the Rockies and fished in the Gulf, partnered in land schemes in Oregon, were in fact inseparable. But when Justin proposed that they set forth on a greater adventure—working their way around the world on freighters—the camaraderie hit a snag. Justin had no family ties but Irwin's parents had been pressuring him to settle down and take his place in his father's bank. The choice was further complicated by Irwin's infatuation with a San Francisco debutante to whom he had proposed. Separation from Justin was painful. Vivid letters from exotic ports increased the pain. Justin even wrote a book called *From Job to Job Around the World,* which I discovered one summer in my grandfather's bookcase, well-thumbed and fondly inscribed to my father.

For his last call to adventure Justin had proposed that he and Irwin enlist together in the AEF, go to France and show those Huns where to get off. This outraged Olga. Not only did Irwin have ample exemptions with job and family, but she was not about to tolerate his deserting her to go shooting Germans.

The day after learning of Justin's death Irwin, without informing Olga, enlisted in the army and requested duty in the machine-gun corps. Before he could be called up, the Armistice was signed (on the day after my fifth birthday). Irwin took the Armistice as a personal frustration and several times came home rowdy drunk. Then I came home from kindergarten with the influenza virus.

The epidemic victimized everyone in the household except the German cook. Pneumonia complicated my mother's condition. My baby brother barely survived. It was my husky handsome father who perished. Since I was the first to recover I was the last member of the family to see him alive. In defiance of doctor's orders and nurse's protests he had dragged himself from his sickbed, determined to go downtown to his office. Passing the bathroom I saw him at the basin honing his razor. He smiled weakly and sighed and urged me to do things like stay well and be good and grow up big. I ran forward and grabbed his leg and held on until he bent down and gave me a kiss that left lather on my cheek. I didn't wipe it off.

He was brought home in an ambulance and died in the night without regaining consciousness.

*

*A*side from forcing us to sing "O Tannenbaum" and "Silent Night" on Christmas Eve the only verse I associate with my mother is "This Little Pig Went to Market." Once in a while at my baby bedtime she would chant this rhyme as she tweaked my toes one by one until she reached "This little pig went squeak squeak squeak all the way home." I wondered if my toes were the only thing she liked about me. Olga had a fixation on feet. Maybe because both of her middle toes were abnormally long.

Did any of this influence the poem I wrote years later?

Papa has a pig.
And a big pig too.
Papa plays a piggy-toe that I can't do.
O papa has the biggest pig you ever did see.
He gave only ten little piggies to me.
　　　　Papa has the star of all the swine,
　　　　Papa shines stern in the sty, &c.

This actually was written about my stepfather, who was

the biggest pig I knew as a child. I also wrote one about my mother, which begins:

> What a big nose Mrs. Mother has,
> the better to smell her dear.
> Sniff sniff sniff it comes round the door,
> detective of anything queer…

She was always checking us for boy crimes and misdemeanors, checking whether we had moved our bowels or said our prayers or parked chewing gum under the table. My own secret prayer began:

> Now I lay me down to sleep,
> I pray the Lord to help me out.
> I'm flat on my back and left alone.
> So God bless nobody, please keep out…

Unlike my grandmother Jennie, who sent me a missal and a hymnal bound in soft leather when I was confirmed at St. Paul's in San Rafael, my mother never showed any interest in my spiritual development. In Olga's family the prime usefulness of the Almighty, if invoked seriously, was to help one make money.

*

I resented being made to smile at prospective stepfathers. I had forever lost the chance to laugh enough with my real father. Not surprisingly, I moped more than I smiled. Sometimes I couldn't restrain my tears. This annoyed my mother: "What a namby-pamby sissy. One look at you and you start boohooing. You're just too sensitive for this world. If you don't quit this sulking I'll give you something to really cry about."

Any self-respecting poet would have felt too sensitive for my mother's world. Convinced that I was a liability in the eyes of any he-man suitor, Olga would introduce me as some pitiable mistake of nature. She never understood that sissies like poets are tougher than they look, that they learn early to sidestep and outwit and endure, that they giggle rather than growl because, being pariahs, they are free to laugh at the delusions of the world and to kiss the joys as they fly.

THE PLAYGROUND

A Play for Precarious Grownups (Complete)

THE PLAYGROUND: A PLAY FOR PRECARIOUS GROWNUPS

The verse-drama *The Playground* (1949) was James Broughton's first published book. The play first appeared in *Theatre Arts* magazine in 1946. In *Coming Unbuttoned* Broughton says that he wrote the play "in response to Hiroshima and the apprehensions that followed. It mocked people who bury their heads in the sand when the fate of the planet is at stake." With his friend Kermit Sheets, Broughton co-founded Centaur Press, "... which we operated for five years ... We intended to print volumes by all our poet friends, but mine of course was to be the first":

I learned to set type, and to throw it, while Kermit sweated over the make-ready and inking. Luckily [printer] Adrian Wilson lived in the flat above our basement press room: he could be called down to disentangle a snafu. Ever since that first volume I have most cherished the books I have had a hand in physically shaping.

When *The Playground* came back from the bindery we invited everyone we knew to a publication party. Our narrow flat was so crowded that John Cage and Merce Cunningham never made it up the stairs. Elsewhere the book was ignored, but we sold enough copies that first night to cover the costs of edition. At thirty-five I was euphoric over my first literary offspring. At thirty-five Whitman published *Leaves of Grass*, Mozart wrote *The Magic Flute*, Byron finished *Don Juan*, Buddha was enlightened, and I held in my hand a verse play of thirty-five pages.

Kermit's production of *The Playground* at the Interplayers ran for months.

THE PLAYGROUND

A Play for Precarious Grownups

The Persons in the Play

The Rompers

The Men on the Seesaw
The Women in the Swing
The Couple on the Slide
The Sun Bather
The Man on the Pogo Stick

The Spoil-sports

The Balloon Man
The Ice Cream Girl
The Handy Boy

The Game-keepers

The Recreation Inspector
The Secretary of the Mausoleum
The Three Geometrists

The Time and The Place

*T*he scene resembles a large city playground in a park. However, all the usual apparatus and amusements look somewhat unusual here. Rising from the center of the wading pool is a pillar, upon which stands the bust of a blackbird crowned with laurel. The entrance gate has no fence or wall, but flags fly from its posts. In mid-air dangles a green traffic light, and also a string of lanterns. All of these are lit, for it is difficult to tell whether it is morning or dusk. Actually, the time is about now and shortly thereafter. When the action begins, it has already been going on for some time. There are two businessmen going up and down on a seesaw. There are two luncheon ladies swinging in a swing. A husband and wife are polishing and dusting the slide.

MEN ON THE SEESAW

See saw
marginal law
O how will I be my own master?
If I put down a penny a day
will I go up any faster?

Either or
lesser or more
O what will supply my demand?
How can I eat my valuable cake
and keep it alive in my hand?

WOMEN IN THE SWING

The pickle was sour, so I bought a flower.
The flower was dead, so I bought a thread.
The thread was thin, so I bought a pin.
The pin was sharp, so I bought a harp.
    But a harp's so difficult to play!

THE COUPLE ON THE SLIDE

Up-the-spout roundabout lickety split-side!
We have a slide with a tickly sit-ride!

RECREATION INSPECTOR

(with a clipboard)

I am the Inspector of Recreation.
I compile and file data on the status of play
for the domestic policy of the Mausoleum.
The apparatus here shows mounting depreciation
while the operating methods remain the same.
But I only report, I have nothing to say.

> *(The Sun Bather undulates gravely to the wading-pool and undresses. She applies lotions as she lolls.)*

SUN BATHER

The unfound bone that sticks in the teeth
the petrified lump that swims in the throat,
not there not there but always there:
    Anxiety, abide with me!

The spider pinch the itch of flea
that cannot be found under the sleeve,
not there not there, but always there:
    Abide with me, anxiety!

The scratch the sting the burn the twitch
always a crawl to infect the flesh
somewhere not there but always there:
    O anxiety, abide with me!
    Abide with me, anxiety!

> *(The Ice Cream Girl runs in and out among the*

apparatus. She carries two pink cones.)

ICE CREAM GIRL

O laughing, my lover, where come you, where lie?
I could lap you so lovely, I care not to die.

O loving, my laughter, where come you, where lie?
I could lip you so lively, I can bear not to die.

(She runs away, searching.)

MAN ON THE POGO STICK

(jerking by)

One plus one is one too many.
One plus one is one too many.

ALL THE ROMPERS

(pressing around the slide)

The last down the slide is unfit to be tied!
The last down the slide is undignified!

*(A warning bell jangles. The green traffic light
flashes yellow.)*

RECREATION INSPECTOR

I have nothing to say but I'll have to report
the sand in your slide-box is turning to mud.
Look where you stand, look where you'll land.
The sand in your slide-box has turned to mud.

ROMPERS

(scurrying in alarm)

What will we do? We must have it fixed!

RECREATION INSPECTOR

I merely inspect, I simply report.
I handle nothing but data.

ROMPERS

Handy Boy, Handy Boy! Where is the Handy Boy?
Who'll write a protest to the Mausoleum?
What will we do if our slide doesn't fit right?

WOMEN IN THE SWING

And a sharp's so difficult to play!

*(The Balloon Man, making his rounds, jauntily
pokes his head into the circle.)*

BALLOON MAN

Have you been readying the barometers lately?
It is darker than you think!
Have you the right bright balloon handy?
Have you the right moon bright for the route you are going?

ROMPERS

(recoiling)

Commit no nuisance upon this property!
Do not disturb, do not enter here.

*(The traffic light goes out. A pennant on the gate
blows away. The Rompers fret.)*

BALLOON MAN

The average sleepwalker is the youngest of 5 1/2 brothers.
Am I the only one who minds the weatherman?

*(A flourish of trumpets. The Secretary of the
Mausoleum bustles in. All the Rompers crowd
around him.)*

ROMPERS

To the Honorable the Secretary of the Mausoleum:
Dear Mr. Secretary: Respectfully yours:
Why are we bothered by the light going out,
defects in the drainage and loose ventilation?

SECRETARY

Dear Sir: Dear Madam: Gentlemen:
We regret the repairs do not exceed the damage.
Use the apparatus at your own risk.
This property has been condemned.

ROMPERS

Condemned? Condemned? How can that be?
Disturbing the peace is against the law.

SECRETARY

My Dear Sir: My Dear Madam:
We have to consider the following points:
a)   the safety of the investment
b)   the net return
c)   quick marketability
d)   the redemption rate.

ROMPERS

But nothing must teeter our status of quo!
Will our Ostrich holdings go up or down?
O anxiety, abide with me now!

SECRETARY

Ladies: Gentlemen:
There is no cause for undue alarm.
The elected Menders of the Mausoleum are in session.
I give you assurance from the Pres. And the Vice Pres.
plus solemner nods of the Sec. and the Treas.
that everything possible is being done
ad lib ad lib ad infinitum
to find a way to make Peace pay.

ROMPERS

Commit no nuisance upon this security. We cannot be

responsible for fire or theft.

SECRETARY

In reply to same
permit me to say
as per your request
the contents noted,

At the present writing
we beg to advise
in due course
we will keep you posted.

Yours truly
very truly your
yours very truly
yours yours yours!

> *(He bustles out. Another pennant falls from the gate.)*

BALLOON MAN

(following the Secretary out)

What do the Menders mend in their Mausoleum?
Have they the right bright signal handy?
Have they a climbing parachute ready?
And the peace that passeth through all understanding?

SUN BATHER

O Anxiety, now my pool is drying up!
There'll be nothing left but a gooey slime!

ROMPERS

Handy Boy, Handy Boy, where is the Handy Boy?
Who'll fix our box, who'll patch our pool?
We'll never sit tight if we cannot slide!

RECREATION INSPECTOR

I merely inspect, I simply report.

> *(He saunters away, continuing on his tour.)*
> *(Left alone, the Rompers solemnly circle the pool*
> *and address a hymn to the bust of the blackbird.)*

ROMPERS

Raven of the small hazard, O
abbreviate our palpitation
our irritating perturbation,
O gentle crow of the little request
can you diminish the chronic worries
flapping alarm over our nests?

The shiver and throb behind our ears
threaten symptoms of large disease:
delete the slight weakening in our knees
   O please
deliver us from our minor fears!

Raven O of the very small hazard
alleviate our trepidation
the strain of daily consternation.
O genteel god of the tiny wrath
can you dispel the vulture flurries
over our therapeutic baths?

> *(They march out, chanting)*

O Raven O!

> *(The Handy Boy enters briskly with a ladder. He*
> *nimbly mounts it and sets about repairing the dark*
> *traffic light.)*

HANDY BOY

I can spruce, I can furbish,

I can shipshapes achieve.
And to wake up the woebegone
I have hopes up my sleeve.
But the long wrong world sleeps late, sleeps late.

I tinker, I tender
no delights that deceive.
For the trick to be trumped up
I've no card up my sleeve.
But the long wrong world sleeps late, sleeps late.

I will rig, I will outfit
the bright joys to believe.
And to hoist a high merriment
I will roll up my sleeve.
But the long wrong world sleeps late, sleeps late.

(The Ice Cream Girl comes skipping back with one pink and white double-decker cone. She offers it to the Handy Boy.)

ICE CREAM GIRL

O laughing, my lover, where come you, where lie?
I could lap you so lovely, I care not to die.

O loving, my laughter, where come you, where lie?
I could lip you so lively, I can bear not to die.

Come tense me, my due love, tense me and claim:
the world's bloody raiment weaves me a chain.

Come clench me, my new love, propensity claim:
the oxen of murder are calling my name.

O densely, my true love, come ripe and renew:
the aged are endless, the newborn are true.

(They embrace and dance.)

MAN ON THE POGO STICK

(jerking past again)

One plus one is one too many.
One minus one isn't any.

>   *(A sound of shattering glass. The Balloon Man*
>   *returns and addresses the   Lovers, who take up*
>   *the chorus.)*

BALLOON MAN

Blessed are the peacemakers
for they shall be called the children of

In the duly elected mausoleum of the split-hair minds
mummy trophies clutter the marble halls,
obscure the view of the memorial inscriptions
and are usually dusty.
Mice find the walls too chilly for siestas,
sparrows do not risk a fall from the flying buttress
and pigeons dubiously bespot the balustrade.

Blessed are the peacemakers
for they shall be called the children

However
interesting things have been known to happen in mausoleums:
the dead have been known to rise from the grave
(we are told) and walk,
even upon a memorable occasion
ascending to the Right Hand.

Blessed are the peacemakers
for they shall be called the

Otherwise

since miracles are still mechanically imperfect
it is more likely these dead, if they walk at all,
ambulate only as ambiguous ghosts among th
This phenomenon, though rather less interes...
titillates the tourists of the macabre.

    Blessed are the peacemakers
    for they shall be called

However
it is not enough
for bodiless heads of state
to float round the rubbernecks like cloudy owls.
This is not enough
when out of the busts in the hall of fame
a sawdust sediment is dripping.
Something really interesting must happen in this mausoleum.
Otherwise —

    Blessed are the peacemakers
    for they shall be

Nor is it enough
merely to fumigate the rooms,
truck the trophies out to the grinding company,
poison the rats that have gnawed the marble.
This will have to be the final funeral of the grave-diggers,
the at last undertaking of the true task,
the wide wakening of the asylum of sleep.
Otherwise –

    Blessed are the peacemakers
    for they shall

In the mausoleum of the split-hair minds
the roof will have to be cracked wide
and the dead arise from the grave,

embody the miraculous wing of breath,
release the true unpoliceable dove,
(O we have been told for centuries)
cut loss the cord of the ascendable parachute
into wonder-embracing flight out of all dusty tombs.
Interesting things like these must happen in the mausoleum.
Otherwise —

  Blessed are the peacemakers
  for they

  for they shall be called
  and called and called

  they are the children of

MAN ON THE POGO STICK

(jolting in and halting)

One plus one is one too many.
One minus one isn't any.
One over one is apt to fall.

    *(He moves the ladder near the Raven's pillar and
    cautiously climbs it.)*

    *(The Rompers renter, wearing rose-covered
    glasses.)*

WOMEN OF THE SWING

(unable to make it budge)

The pickle is thin, and so is the flower.
Now our swing is too difficult to play!

MEN OF THE SEESAW

(finding it stuck on the horizontal)

No margin to master? No up and down faster?
O supply! O demand!
Which will consume the cake or the hand?

SUN BATHER

(discovering a teeter in the pillar)

The pillar is loose, the Raven may spill.
O please, Anxiety, abide with me still!

ROMPERS

Handy Boy, Handy Boy! Hurry and patch!
Swab out our slide, prop up our pool!
We mustn't be left with a gooey slime!

> *(They chase away the Ice Cream Girl and pull the
> Handy Boy about.*
>
> *A siren wails.*
>
> *The ladder falls from under the Man with the
> Pogo Stick.)*

RECREATION INSPECTOR

(returning, matter-of-factly)

I am obliged to add an emergency report
of a slight alteration in normal service.
Due to a minor power shortage
the reservoir fire is out of control,
is spreading through the zoological gardens,
and has already capsized the model home.

SECRETARY

(puffing in)

Dear Sir: Dear Madam: To Whom It May Concern:
We are doing everything in our power.
We are reopening the Bureau of Missing Persons
in the unfinished new wing of the Municipal Pet Shop.
Yours very truly, yours yours yours!

> *(He scoots out, taking the Handy Boy.)*

ROMPERS

(panicky)

O where is the key to my safe-deposit?
How do I get to the Travelers Aid?
Is there a weatherproof case for the Raven?
And who will look after the Ostriches?
O where can the Ostriches stay?

BALLOON MAN

There are no available vacancies for headless hermits
now that the earthquake moon has burst on the desert
and the roadbeds are hot with ruin and rust.
Who will go running again upon their plumed behinds?
There are no down payments obtainable
for snug sandy islands in this scalded over-boiled sea.

If you are considering other possible long necks
this is not even a good time for swans.
How serene can they float in an overturned tempest?
How clear are the air-lanes for geese over volcanoes?
Flamingoes appear merely incongruous
after the sandstorm scorches the jungle.

And where will your defeathered friends find a furnishable room
in the molten dust after the eruption?
There are no more life-rafts for light housekeeping.
There are no permanent addresses with a view of the morass.
Perhaps here and there, if you come early and stand in line,
a shifting lava bed, transient, on a daily rate.

So maybe the ostrich has had his eye on a good thing:
maybe the grave new world is the underworld.
Shall we then scrabble under the ruins
down to the nether no-weather realms,
bedfellow the worm, woo the mole,
and dwell in the dark among the decapitated ostrich heads?

ROMPERS

Do not disturb! Keep quiet, keep clear!
We cannot be responsible for fire and death.
Loud-mouth peddler! Keep out of here!

> *(They chase off the Balloon Man. Thunder. The
> Gate sags. The Rompers scatter, covering their
> ears with mittens.)*

MAN ON THE POGO STICK

One plus one is one too many.
One minus one isn't any.
One over one is apt to fall.
One by itself is the best of all!

> *(He crawls into the sandbox and digs until he
> disappears.)*

> *(The Ice Cream Girl, blindfolded, her hands tied
> behind her, wanders helpless and lost among the
> apparatus. The Handy Boy goes to her rescue and
> comforts her.)*

HANDY BOY

O in the time
that shall be that must be
the time of Ever (if ever)
when birds shall be wings again
and the weather all Now:

From the trumpets the drum
the applause over dust
from all the yelping tin hounds
O come with me come
away to the silence neglected,
come quest with me quietly
to a morning coast.

For then shall be time the time

to waken the wild dove's sleep again
the golden finch at the sea again,
O then must be the time (if ever)
to reopen our sound-broken eyes
anew at the bird forest
reenter the singing green weather.

And there will I show you
see! all Now on the earth
(O will I? will you be there?)
from the Ever surf look! to the pines
in the Here air O! in the everywhere light
O look beloved look! my heart.

> *(Trumpet flourish, triumphant. The Rompers
> reassemble, in earmuffs. The Secretary struts in,
> grandiloquent.)*

SECRETARY

Ladies and Men, Women and Gents:
the emergency situation has been completely modified.
We are about to enter a new scientific period
of reimproved Mausoleum security.
It is now my great pleasure to present to you
The Big Three Geometrists Glee Club.

> *(The Three Geometrists pace solemnly in and set
> up elaborate instruments. The Balloon Man follows
> at a distance.)*

1st GEOMETRIST

Behold and admire! We clarify the unclearable!
We repair warped circles, we dissect bent diameters,
we remodel unworkable surds in powdered blue.
Never mind the thrush locked in the basement:
we are experts in the short division of fractures
on the longest distance between many ungiven points.
Render unto us your square pegs, your round holes,

your ruptured perpendiculars and aging radii:
we cut every indivisible down to pi.

TRIO

We are making a new world Q. E. D.

2nd GEOMETRIST

Give us this day your acutely tangled triangle,
we will operate on all the tangents.
Never mind the weather or the tree upstairs:
disrobe the elusive knots of your ellipse,
relax your lumpy circumference for surgery,
we will disinfect the unequilateral spots.
The ether is cubic on the logarithm table:
with our sharp quotient and slide ruler
we will now extract the roots of your hypotenuse.

TRIO

We are making a new world Q. E. D.

3rd GEOMETRIST

Behold, admire and rejoice! O convalesce!
In spite of the rain and the tree in the attic
in spite of the birds bolted in the boiler room,
we have decapitated the unreliable exile x,
assassinated the collaborating satellite y,
imprisoned the ungovernable nth power,
and permanently severed relations with infinity
down to an accurate one two-thousandth of an inch.
Alleluia! Find your symmetrical dot on the graph!

TRIO

We are making a new world Q. E. D.

> *(The Rompers applaud. The Geometrists shake
> hands with one another.)*

BALLOON MAN

Blessed are the peacemakers!

ROMPERS

Up-the-spout roundabout quickety split-wide.
We'll have a new slide with a delicate sit-ride!

BALLOON MAN

When split-hair minds put their heads in split-second huddles
how can the really interesting thing happen in the mausoleum?
Am I the lonely one who minds the Weatherman?

> (The red traffic light clangs and flashes. A sudden
> blinding explosion. All the apparatus in the
> Playground rocks dizzily and falls askew.)

ROMPERS

My sit! My ride! O my abide!
Our property props! O slide!

RECREATION INSPECTOR

(returning)

The interruption in normal service will continue indefinitely.
An unchainable reaction has occurred in the Security
Laboratories.
The Mausoleum has sunk with all its Menders.

SECRETARY

Under the circumstances
I hereby tender my resignation.
Yours very truly!

> (He flees, flanked by the Geometrists.)

ROMPERS

O status! O quo! Where can we go?
Where is our new world Q. E. D.?

(Darkness. A cold wind blows up.)

BALLOON MAN

What are you taking into the Dark Ages?
Do you think your umbrella is warm enough?
How are you preparing for the imminent tunnel
at the approaching fork in the road?

You had best be warned to expect
a little more than the usual discomforts of traveling,
and customary whims of the weather
and the unsanitary conditions of foreign lands.
The forecast for mornings is generally mouldy
and the nights will last from three weeks to a century and a half.

What are you taking with you into the Dark Ages?
Will you bundle up in your furry scar tissue,
button up well in your woolly political issues?
How many trunks have you packed?

Reservations cannot be obtained in advance
and meals are not being served in the summer dining room
  on the American plan
due to conditions beyond our control.
It is also likely that the ballroom will remain boarded up.
However, coronary thrombosis will be provided daily
through the courtesy of the management
at no additional cost.

So, what are you taking into the long winter evenings?
There are no round-trip tickets on this short-circuit express
and the itinerary does not even promise to be scenic,
but the stopover privilege is permanent.
How are you planning to impress the worms?

You had better not rely on the fortuitous conjunction
with Venus in your horoscope;
you might as well abandon

the insurance policy in the icebox,
the savings-account in the jelly closet:
what value will your nest-egg be
(even from your goldenest goose)
to what possible Museum of Natural History?

Locking the portmanteau at the last moment,
have you forgotten anything?
Are you sure?
In your vanity case which is your essential elixir?
Did you remember the one item that never needs ironing,
   moth balls, or keys?

Did you overlook the single imperative
for the traveler on perilous journeys?
Did it occur to you as you checked your final list?
Do you even know what it is?

> (*A shivering silence. The wind howls. The Raven's
> pillar falls limp.*)

ROMPERS

> (*whimpering together*)

It mustn't get dark!
I'll lose myself!
I'll catch my death!

> (*The Handy Boy and the Ice Cream Girl quickly
> cross the Playground toward the Gate.*)

BALLOON MAN

Handy Boy! Ice Cream Girl!
What are you taking into the Dark Ages?
Do you have the method for a new moon ready?
Can you light the right flare for a weather-wise route?

HANDY BOY

The long wrong world sleeps late, sleeps late.

But to wake up the woebegone
I can roll up my sleeve.
And to hoist a high merriment
I have hopes up my sleeve.

(The Balloon Man fervently apostrophizes the lovers.)

BALLOON MAN

One and wonder are the flags for splendor's signal.
            How?
        When eyes behold from I am One
then bright unveil the semaphores at the mist mast.
So ponder might wonder not wider be done
        to make One indivisible
                now
for all blinded and blundering brutal and sundered.

        Might it explosively fly
to light the untrimmable wick in the will
reheat the mildewing beam in the brain
and the flickering bicker-damp heart?
        White as one luminous eye
ignite the steaming dim and the dark?

O to see a world made firmament of whirling beacons
                grow
        when the eyes of all men
kindle firm lighthouse from ever socket,
sweep wide the blind night with far sighting
        for wonder-working Ones.
                Lo!
What rocket pivoting beholding boldness all afire!

ICE CREAM GIRL

O laughing, my lover, come take me, come fly.
I will love you so lively, we shall fear not to die.

(With assurance the lovers prepare to depart.)

BALLOON MAN

Otherwise—
This will be the Darkest Age of all time!

ALL THE ROMPERS

(angrily encircling him)

Loud-mouth peddler! Meddler! Lout!
You are the gummer of all the works!
Humbug bugaboo! Out! Out! Out!

> *(Furiously they attack the Balloon Man. He falls to the ground, slain. The Handy Boy, running to the rescue, can save only one of the balloons.*
>
> *Earthquake. Thunder and darkness. The Playground collapses. The Rompers race to the toppling slide.)*

ROMPERS

(pushing and scrambling)

Me! No me! Let me!
Does it still fit? Does it still fit?
Ouchy ouchy, rickety split!
Whee! Whee! Whee!

> *(They slide down in various positions of hysterical despair, and one by one disappear into the sandbox at the bottom.)*

RECREATION INSPECTOR

(as he departs)

I merely inspect, I have nothing to retort.
There is nothing to say with everything said.
There is nothing but the report:

HANDY BOY AND ICE CREAM GIRL

(alone, beside the Balloon Man's body)

O in the time that shall be that must be
the time to reenter the singing green weather
    beholding boldness all afire:
Come widely with true love, come ripe and renew.
The cages are mendless, the reborn are due.

> *(The balloon held by the Handy Boy lights up in*
> *the darkness.)*

The Androgyne Journal

THE ANDROGYNE JOURNAL

(1991 VERSION)
(COMPLETE)

The Androgyne Journal is one of James Broughton's central utterances. The journal form itself is a deeply American one, calling to mind writers such as Thoreau and Emerson, both of whom Broughton admired. Written in 1960, when the poet was forty-seven, the book deals with what he called "a bewildering adventure in my life," "an often inexplicable experience." It was first published in 1977 by Scrimshaw Press of Oakland. Broughton revised the text for its second publication by Broken Moon Press in 1991. *The Androgyne Journal* bears a close relationship to one of Broughton's most Jungian films, *Dreamwood*, released in 1972, and I want to introduce the book somewhat indirectly by some remarks about the film. In both film and book the primary theme is self-acceptance—but it is also necessary to redefine the self that one is accepting.

The Bed (1968) Broughton's first color film, had been filmed during San Francisco's 1967 "Summer of Love." It was only 20 minutes long, but it was an explosion of energy and imagination. Featuring the attractions of naked bodies and the Northern California landscape as well as such friends and local celebrities as Alan Watts, Imogen Cunningham, Grover Sales and Jean Varda, the film was a great success and rejuvenated Broughton's sagging career as a director. His next film was *Nuptiae* (1969), a celebration of the poet's marriage to Suzanna Hart. In *Nuptiae* Jungian themes—as well as the idea of film as "ritual" rather than self-expression or comedy—become not only explicit but dominant. *Dreamwood*, filmed like *The Bed* in and around Druid Heights, Marin County, is, at 46 minutes, the longest of Broughton's films. "This homage to Cocteau," writes Broughton, "flows from my own poet's blood and unfolds in the cadences of mythic ritual." Here is his description of the film's "apparitional narrative":

> [S]omewhere (at the center of the world) there is an island called Animandra, or the Kingdom of Her. And somewhere

in the wilds of Animandra there is a magic wood known as Broceliande, the Perilous Forest. Within this labyrinthine grove the dreamwood mysteries take place, the tests, the encounters, the rites of the Goddess in her many forms. Only a hero dares risk his life by entering this realm of the feminine powers. And most heroic is the poet, perhaps, guided as he is (and taunted) by that blessed damozel, his muse, whose name is Alchemina. Ordinary men remain safely outside in the dry meadows of their masculine games. But to the man who conquers his fear, persists in his quest and wins her favor, the Goddess of Dreamwood will reveal her greatest secret.

What might have been in another poet the descent into hell becomes for Broughton the entrance into "the realm of the feminine powers"— and, as the allegorical names suggest, his hero's adventures take a decidedly Jungian turn. In her essay on the process of "individuation," the Jungian analyst Marie-Louise von Franz asserts that "the character of a man's anima"—the "feminine" side of a man's unconscious—"is as a rule shaped by his mother":

If he feels that his mother had a negative influence on him, his anima will often express itself in irritable, depressed moods, uncertainty, insecurity, and touchiness…. The whole of life takes on a sad and oppressive aspect. Such dark moods can even lure a man to suicide, in which case the anima becomes a death demon. She appears in this role in Cocteau's film *Orphee*.

Even without the reference to Cocteau, one can see the relevance of this to Broughton. Broughton's mother appears as "the negative mother-anima figure" in *Mother's Day, The Androgyne Journal,* and *Dreamwood.* Von Franz goes on to describe "the anima in her proper positive role … as mediator between the ego and the Self":

> *This positive function occurs when a man takes seriously the feelings, moods, expectations, and fantasies sent by his anima and when he fixes them in some form—for example, in writing, painting, sculpture, musical composition, or dancing…. And it is essential to regard it as being absolutely real; there must be no lurking doubt that this is "only a fantasy."*

"Under certain conditions," writes Jung himself, "the unconscious spontaneously brings forth an archetypal symbol of wholeness." The Androgyne is precisely such a symbol, and Broughton's work abounds in both literal and metaphorical references to it. One might postulate that there is a continual tension in Broughton between the person who needs another—and whose longing at times seems endless—and the totally self-sufficient individual. This tension finds expression (and, to some extent, resolution) in the figure of the Androgyne, which is at once "double"— two—and "singular"—one.

The concluding images of *Dreamwood* arise out of these contrary tensions. As Broughton describes his intention, the hero experiences "unity" and then:

turns and slowly rises, finding himself in a totally different place—between forest and meadow. And he is radiant in the sunlight. And as he stands we can see that within him is the body of a woman fully contained and at peace.

Standing fully erect, with this inner living miracle contained inside him, he opens out his arms.

[The] image of union and unity achieved is seen...

In his early work Broughton could oppose the forces of death only with such energy as he could find in his passion for his medium. Here he has found a figure, a person, a venerable symbol—"a bisexual being"—which also embodies such energy. He calls that figure "the Ineffable Lollapalooza," "the Divine Androgyne." 'Standing fully erect"—like baby James in his crib—the Androgyne is at once Broughton himself, a narcissistic projection of his own psyche into the world, and something totally external to himself: the god Hermes, whom the poet describes as "the god of poets, doctors and thieves ... messenger of the gods and of the godbody in the phallus ... every man's pride, embarrassment and joy." The "happy ending" of most films is the image of a marriage: the lonely man and woman simultaneously find each other and happiness. The reason for this conception of happiness is that the culture at large "explains" loneliness as the desire for a mate: find someone, get married, reproduce, consume as much as possible, die. Broughton's hero begins by chasing after a woman, but instead of marrying her he "incorporates" her. It is not for another but for himself that the hero seeks:

> Come live with me and be my life
> and we shall have no need of wife.
> ("75 Life Lines")

Like everything Broughton produced, *The Androgyne Journal* is an instance of his extraordinary ability to mythologize experience. In *Picturing Cultural Values in Postmodern America*, William G. Doty describes the "writer" in terms that fit Broughton and *The Androgyne Journal* perfectly:

> *What is… a "writer" for, if not to link together our aspirations and our sorrows, our ecstasy and our tragedy into patterns that transcend the merely personal? In the process the writer reestablishes and refounds the language from the disconnected bits that have become only randomly chaotic: hence the process of writing or interpreting is a creative process of ordering analogous to the cosmogonic feats of the primordial times, and it becomes difficult to avoid the "religious" quality of writing or myth making as such: … religare (from which English religion most likely is derived) also means etymologically tying things into a ligature or bundle of meanings.*
>
> *Perhaps that is why so many creation myths feature creation by the divine word, thought, dream, laughter, or fantasy: what one learns from such myths is not the status of particular sets of deities but how to function as a creator, how to speak into coherence those bits of language mud, those discarded shards of metaphor, that can only be combined at this time and place.*

One might also compare what Broughton experiences here to what Jack Kerouac described in his novel, Big Sur—especially the way each of these writers conceives of the Pacific Ocean.

THE ANDROGYNE JOURNAL

JUNE 23
Cuffey's Cove

Why am I really here? To hide myself away, or to burst open?

I anticipated a quiet retreat. But each day the creature inside me becomes more demanding. How can I accept the needs of this double-sexed being that lives in me? There is no denying its reality. I can touch it directly and feel it throb. At any moment I can put one hand on Her and one on Him. Then my body grows urgent, and so do I. Wildly so. How can I control this erupting mystery?

I am sitting at the open window of this small cabin. Wild roses and nasturtiums surround it. The cliff drops below me to the sea. The air reverberates with hummingbirds and insects, with boom of surf and sheep-bleat from the meadow. What a change from the city—my musty cell in the theater attic. Already I have lost interest in revising my play. I am too excited. I have been invaded by my own secrets and I must try to find out how to live with them.

Has this phenomenon always dwelt in me? The hermaphrodite as a symbol of wholeness has fascinated me since childhood. I am surprised how few men condone the image of it, let alone accept it as a clue to their souls. But now that I am experiencing the volatile paradox in my own body I am astonished. When Hermes and Aphrodite encounter inside me and create a new creature there, a new Hermaphroditus, the ecstasy of inner union overwhelms me.

How did this happen? Some years ago I became aware of an intense life in my nipples. Touching them aroused my genitals more than any other self-play act. At the time I thought this odd and rather shameful. The sensitivity, however, intensified and deepened. Now the urge has become exhilarating instead of shameful. Now in my male breasts I can directly touch my female heart, I can touch the curving, yielding, love-giving Lady of my Soul. I have but to stroke my nipples tenderly and at once she responds to my caress. Then she wakens the He in me. My penis asserts a thrust like the burning roar of the Alchemical Lion. Spontaneous magic!

Wasn't this wakening of my nipples the way I discovered the form of my own hermaphrodite? Always I had wondered why men retain vestigial nipples. Now I no longer question. They are not vestigial, they are palpable doors to the chamber of the Goddess. She is present in every man's breast. She lives in every man's womb.

JUNE 24

I am grateful to Bill. In this weathered pine cabin I will be undisturbed. I need only to be up at the inn to help out at mealtimes. Spacious silence and rugged beauty surround me here. Will I begin a new life? Or have a meaningful death? In this noble landscape one might be resurrected handsomely.

Today I registered for a morning class at the Art Center in Mendocino. For a change I will try to portray only what I see in front of me. I will try to anchor myself in outer reality. I will try to become a child again observing the world for the first time.

Is the real rose as believable as the imaginary rose?

*   *   *

I have spent most of the afternoon sitting among the stones and the driftwood down at the cove. I sift the stones, wondering at their solidarity and form. How will I ever be able to be as specific as a stone? Will my secrecies ever be that forthright?

Sifting pebbles through my fingers I ask vital questions of the Sea. If all that a stone is expected to be is the stone that it is, why isn't a man expected to be the kind of man that he is instead of someone's idea of what man he should be?

This rockbound cove is a fine private place. It has a steep path down to it through poison oak and cannot be seen from the inn. It has grottoes and a cave. Here the Sea becomes an intimate presence. Here is a Sea one can speak to and be heard..

I would like to toss into the waves every uncertainty. I would like the Sea to wash away all my denials. I have had too many years of superficial Lents and never a genuine crucifixion. Will I ever dare to stand before the wind stripped utterly down to me? Will I ever accept that I contain many men and many women trying to live together?

*   *   *

In the night two Navajo midwives came and removed the bolt on the door to the tower in my head. And the princess came down. She came down the stairs from the tower where she had been confined for many years, the young princess who was older than Lilith. When she removed her veil she looked even more enigmatic.

She began stroking my feet. Then she asked what more she might stroke because, she said, she had descended for the sole purpose of being tender to my needs. She said she believed in me so much that she could not bear to leave me untended.

For all your impulses I have the tenderest regard, she said. If it be to play with yourself, to lie with young men, to fondle young women, to sit up all night talking to poets, to be alone or drunk and disorderly, ascetic or gregarious, whatever, that's no blame, no shame. All I ask, she said, is that you touch me so that I can know that I am real.

What is your name? I asked her. Are you Andromeda? Annabel Lee? Anima Mundi?

Call me Ann, if you like.

Are you the Annie I used to invoke as a muse?

Probably.

But when I reached out to touch her, she evaporated.

JUNE 25

I learned in the art class that no two hues have the same value and that the after-image of yellow is blue-violet. I started to draw a cup and an eggbeater on the windowsill but they suddenly turned into a royal couple crowned with a single crown.

Odd, how my experience of the Kingdom of Her and the Queendom of Him comes to me not in any way I expected. It's not an Olympian sideshow, nor an acrobatic Tantra, nor Ariel in the arms of Caliban. It comes instead as exuberant intermingling, as lion and unicorn in gleeful dance, as bosom and genital in conjugal sport, as the equal potency of She in Him and He in Her. Most of all it comes as a recognition that the wedding of male and female in the body creates an androgyne in the soul. Which is like being unexpectedly introduced to undivided Adam.

So wondrous is this that I sit transfixed, staring out at the cypress trees bending in the wind.

* * *

Now I remember how the mystery of the hermaphrodite first challenged me. It was on an afternoon in my ninth year when I opened the bathroom door upon my unsuspecting mother. She stood in the tub directly facing me and I saw that not only did she have the breasts I knew, but below her dark pubic hair there was something more crucial. I had the fleetingest glimpse, because she turned upon me such a murderous glare that I hastily slammed the door and fled to the basement. But I definitely thought I had seen her penis and testicles.

After that she intimidated me more than she already had. I was convinced that she so resented my discovery of her secret power that she would on some dark night annihilate me without warning: not only gouge out my eyes, but cut off my penis and add it to hers.

Hadn't she already disposed of my father? She told me he died in an epidemic when I was five. But I knew better. Didn't she always speak of him with murderous disdain: how she had wanted to get rid of his gym cronies and fraternity brothers, how she could have killed him for running up racing debts and running after fast women?

She was equally disgusted with my acts and appetites. She condemned my pleasure in theatricals, versemaking, belly dancing, movies. Once she whipped me with her riding crop for putting on her pearls. Her customary reply to any whimpering of mine: "You're just too sensitive for this world!" Is this what has dislocated me all these years?

Her retaliation for my seeing her naked was not only unexpected, it was shattering. She sent me away to military school. "To make a man of you," she insisted. I was not yet ten years old. Actually she was planning to marry a man who had even more contempt for me than she did: a self-made bigot dedicated to money, golf and martinis.

In the months after I was put into uniform at the school, where I had to drill every day with a Springfield rifle, I continued to brood on my riddles. Was only a mother a hermaphrodite? Could only a woman be both woman and man? Could I as her son become part woman? Would that make me a more powerful man? In her absence I had tried on her gowns and questioned the result in her dressing room mirror. How was I so different from women, or from other men? Where in the world did I belong? And if not in this world, where else?

My image of the hermaphrodite so obsessed me that I kept drawing it in my notebook during study hall. One evening I was caught red-handed by Lieutenant Joy. He confiscated my notebook. I fled from the schoolroom in tearburst, wept in the washroom, hid in my closet till after taps.

Why did I panic with guilt at that discovery of my secret? Did I fear a violent punishment for revealing the Woman-Man in me? Happily Lieutenant Joy had more sense. He never reported me to the Commandant. He never mentioned the matter to me, nor did he return my notebook. I was too embarrassed to ask him what became of it.

* * *

Maybe my life till now has been totally misguided. A life on a nervous periphery when I thought I was dead center? Why when I am well through my forties do I fear living out what is most real in myself? What old beast squashes my daring?

I am swatted, I am nibbled, I am sat upon. I am a shivering moth in the mouth of this behemoth. Again in this dark night he snorts at me. Having gnawed away all the connective tissue, he is finally eating my vitals.

No, wait! This beast is not a he. It is not my stepfather. It's old She! It's my Cronus Crone, my Saturn Sow. It's my old Mrs. Rhino. She who keeps me on a leash in her sty, she who would have me spayed at the vet's. She says I have no right to my own life. She chases me away from every object I covet. She squelches my desire to paint, to write, to learn the guitar. She spits on my wings. She shits on my laughter.

Annihilate her! Annihilate her!

* * *

When I finally slept Olga my mother came to prepare me for a wedding to the Princess Ann. She and two guardian midwives said they wanted my phallus to enter its rightful domain.

They made me lie down. Instead of the Princess, however, beside me stood a Kahuna King, a powerful and glistening Polynesian bending over me, nude except for a crown of feathers. He had come out of the Pacific to "tone me up," he said, as he pressed his hands into my chest. I was surprised at how malleable his strong fingers were.

To massage every part of my body he climbed over me, his genitals brushing my checks and touching my eyelids. It was as though he wanted to rub all parts of me with the magic his body could communicate, waken me in every limb and chakra, open wider all my orifices. He said he wanted me to acknowledge that I had a tail. Though I realized I was enduring an ordeal,

I felt strong sexual excitement. Olga sat to one side the whole time, beaming her approval.

I reached toward this Kahuna King and grasped his penis and held its thick throbbing heat with my right hand. At that moment on my left Princess Annie appeared, also nude, but now with blonde hair falling to her ankles like a cloak. I reached into her warm honey-dripping vagina. Thus I grasped the sex of both these creatures, to contain them and to unite them in my own body.

JUNE 26

Last night looking out the window into the moonlight I saw the arch through the great rock in the sea. I had a sudden desire to thrust my penis through it. Into, through, and outward—out to the open ocean!

In my dream a long row of mourners sat beside the road on opera chairs. They were waiting for my funeral to pass. They sat rigidly as if holding a pose for a tintype. I hadn't wanted to go to the opera anyway and when it turned out to be Parsifal, I left by the side door and walked past all the bombarded public buildings to get to the garden party where the hostess cautioned me not to pet her sheepdog. He's sore-headed, she said.

O Beloved Androgyne, do not fade! I invoke you again at moonrise. Where have my shinning ones gone?

My bowels are running water. Are they possessed by some volcanic demon who wants to yank me away from what I begin to value? Is Mrs. Rhino trying to get her clout back in? trampling all over my guts?

Hermes! Aphrodite! Stay with me. Keep old Kali Face out of here, we were getting on so well without her! We were just beginning to conceive a saving grace.

Having found my divine parents, I long to be fully reborn. I want to be the enlightened child I always imagined I could be and might at last become. Is my yanking gut pain a birth pang of my new being? Hold him tenderly in his labor, Brother James, you are your own nursling. Rest here within the process of yourself, and rejoice in it.

* * *

Yesterday afternoon I lay on the beach among the stones, feeling their shapes, sifting through them in search of one that would speak to me. I lay beside the ocean roar till the mist rolled in over me and the twilight deepened, lay there outstretched like one of the stones, wanting desperately to be identified with my own form and density. How much time, struggle, and endurance are required of a stone in order for it to become a stone?

Then at almost dark I surprised myself by finding in my hand a stone I did not remember picking up. I knew at once it belonged to me. Shaped like the phallus of an ancient *kouros* it was mottled and veined and was the color of dried blood. I would have known it anywhere: my own Rosetta stone, my fetish, my lapis, my talisman! At last something to hold on to!

This pleased me so much I went weeping and sneezing through the fog as I climbed up the trail back to the inn.

I rub my stone constantly, as if it were a magic lamp. Perhaps it is. Bill says it is a liverstone, not a bloodstone. I say it has a genie who wants me to live. Last night I went to bed with it. I rubbed my navel with it, I rubbed my nipples, I rubbed my phallus. I rubbed all my orifices.

And then I decided to fuck old Mrs. Rhino with it. Having my own stone I no longer feared her. I cornered her on her fringy chaise longue so she could not escape. Like a matador I drove the stone home. The old Sow transformed in my arms. She lay there a delicate maiden, blushing and spilling her strawberries.

Ah! This cove of stones may provide a new beginning. How could I have known that when I went to bed with a stone I would awaken with a wand?

This noon I had my first guitar lesson with Grace Probert. She is a bangled herb lady in the village who once taught school in Sausalito. Even since Carlos sold me his Martin guitar when he married, I have wanted to hear again the mellow sounds it once produced for him. Is there some music of my own that I hope to find in it?

This evening as I was practicing I heard little beasties scamper up and down inside the walls. Now the great circle of the moon climbs the sky on her mysterious rounds. Is there some melodiousness of the feminine that wants to sing through my torso, so to shine there, so to fill the heart?

JUNE 27

I entered a courtyard where men were gathering and greeting as they awaited a signal to enter a cloistered building. These initiates wore full-length robes although their bodies were somehow both naked and clothed at the same time.

The entrance to the cloister had a high double door of ancient design. I was eager to enter with these "brothers" but I wasn't sure I had the right qualifications or knew any password. When a signal was given without my noticing it, the brethren moved toward the entry.

I asked the guardian of the door whether I would be permitted to enter. He said, You have the golden hair, don't you? I didn't know what he meant until I looked down at my right hand. My fingers held a gleaming thread of yellow hair. Amazed and glad I said, Yes! I do!

Inside the building I could see a tall man standing on a podium at the end of a corridor. Toward him all the entrants proceeded. Lithe, broad, and gold-bearded, he was plainly the high priest. For a moment I hesitated. What would I be expected to say to him?

When I glanced back at the guardian of the door he smiled encouragingly. Then I knew my rightful course. I went up to this golden elder in his shining robe, knelt down and whispered, I pray you, Father, give me your blessing.

He looked at me severely. Then he answered me. You can only give the blessing to yourself, my son.

I awoke with the words "prithee, prithee" on my mouth. This dream has excited me.

That golden hair I needed to enter the brotherhood—what else is it but a thread of the glory of my First Beloved, golden Littlejohn of my teen years' passion? His precious yellow hair has been my lost, my impossible desire for a lifetime. And now in my own hand I held his magic. At last I was in touch with him again.

In the military school in San Rafael from my twelfth to my fifteenth year he came to my bed every morning at dawn waking me like a living sunrise, came to make love to me before the other boys awoke, warming my touch, erogenizing me, teaching me how to kiss, how to enjoy being embraced, how to be a lover.

His was a presence of angelic ardor. He was almost albino blond: his curls, his eyebrows, his lashes, his pubic hair were of spun gold, as was the mantle of his firm athlete's body. And that body had an appetizing aroma like that of freshly baked bread flavored with narcissus.

But this, my first love-teacher, was abruptly banished from my life when my mother discovered what sexual passion this schoolmate had aroused in me. She promptly removed me from the school, denouncing my love as evil, criminal and demented. She and my stepfather confined me at home as punishment. There she concentrated on making me believe that the most glorious thing that had ever happened to me was a disgusting and unforgivable sin.

O John, my Littlejohn!

Is not the first vision of love an unforgettable determinant for everyone? Dr. Fenton once told me how his entire life had been conditioned at age fourteen by his having seen from a passing train window a naked youth dive from a cliff into the Eel River.

JUNE 28

Before dawn the two midwives of my rebirth leaned over my cradle in the marsh. One touched my right nipple and one touched my left. By this means they planned to ignite my penis into a fire-stick, which I could rub in the dark belly of the mother whale and so find my way out of her swallow-up. They said I had been prisoner there long enough. Like Spider Woman and Turquoise Woman for a Navajo youth, they would awaken my manhood destiny. First they would bring me back to my hero twin, Littlejohn of the golden hair, from whom I had been separated since age fifteen. Sharing his sunliness again, I could perform my necessary deeds with spurt and laughing.

They had just returned me to the dawntime arrival of my First Beloved, when suddenly the bed changed places, and I was transported to that Los Angeles hotel room of a winter holiday night, years ago in my puberty, when my mother lay beside me sharing the other of the twin beds. I had thought I was playing with myself unobtrusively. But Olga leapt up, yanked back my covers, exposed my happy play to her horror, condemned by depravity and forced me into a shame of tears.

And now, we were there again. But this time she rose approvingly from her bed, came to the side of mine and watched in delight and wonder this man-lover she had given birth to.

O yes, she said, O yes, my son! Let me play with it too! O yes yes, put it into me! Love me with it, inundate me! Ravish me with your and I will give you mine!

Was this the woman who had whipped me for loving myself, for loving another boy, for loving my image dressed in her gowns? She who had locked me up to prevent my loving anyone?

Now I grabbed her, flung her back upon her own bed, and plunged into her triumphantly.

Will I be able to discover my accurate identity only be accepting openly all my guilt-laden epiphanies? Are those ugly-sounding words—masturbation and homosexuality—the actual portals into a reconstituted life? Why are they not better called love-of-self and love-of-comrades?

JUNE 29

Have I come here only to discover how crazy I am? I have

been sitting here for ten minutes trying to swat a fly with a thistle. Will this bearded Venus of mine make everything in life crazier? Where is the right place for such as we? Suppose I can never manage to find it?

I think I will abandon theater work and enter a monastic order.

*   *   *

The night has fallen. I have been on my knees.

To experience the cross and the crossing, the descent and the ascent, the crucifixion redeemed—this desire for transfiguration cries out in my bones. The thighs pinch, the heels pull, the knees twitch, the shoulders wrench. I await the hour, I await the passing over. Only by going all the way to the bottommost pit can one behold the mating dance of Heaven and Hell.

*   *   *

I lay in a tomb as if I had gone down to my ultimate extreme. I lay there awake but unmoving. Then they came to stand on either side of me: the mothers on the left, the fathers on the right, in all their generations.

These were my ancestors who had come to mourn me. They had deep concern in their grieving. Tears fell upon me, like healing waters. I lay as immobile as Jesus in his tomb.

Just then Jesus himself bent over and gave me a loving kiss. Then his father kissed me too. And so followed the other men on my right: my father, grandfather, brother, stepfather, first lover, and guru.

At the same time as each of the men touched my mouth in warm benediction, the women laid hands on my cold body to bring it back to life. They devoted their ritual healing to my shriveled phallus, washing it worshipfully. As it began to stir and to rise, they sang and cheered.

While the women massaged my limbs and torso, the fathers

and brothers came to me again one at a time and each gave me of his own semen to drink that I might be invigorated with the potencies of time. At the fullness of the invigorating my fee rose to the ceiling and my own seed fell into my mouth.

Hallelujah hallelujah! they all sang.

JULY 1

While standing in the swirling waters of the cove, I was stricken with violent nausea. It struck with the agony of unexpected loss, as if my newfound Androgyne had been drowned in an eddy at my feet, not yet able to survive in this world.

I crawled up on the beach and vomited again. I felt devastated, hopelessly alone. Somehow I managed to climb the steep path up the cliff.

When I reached the garden by the inn and smelt the tonic smell of warm earth, a different impulse struck me. I flung myself face down upon the grass, sinking deep into the dry fragrant ground, abandoning to it my body and my pain. Almost at once I felt the Earth's body responding to mine. I began to feel cared for, to feel soothed and healed. Soon I was regenerated enough to sit up with all my burdens restored to me and the world fallen back into place. The sheep were sheep, the sky a sunset glow, the unfinished poem still in my wet knapsack. I could rise and befriend my uncertainties again. It was time to go to work in the dining room.

All the energies in my body flow down through my pelvis as if into a great uterine womb of life. They flow down toward my genitals as if to some fertile delta, and from there flow out into my erect penis, which is the diving board for my headlong plunge into the great inland sea of my own hemisphere.

This delights the orgasmic meeting-mating of Fire into Water and Water back into Fire.

*   *   *

From the kitchen door at sundown I watched the bull in the pasture ecstatically smelling the cow, lifting his intoxicated head into the air as she turned a slow look upon him. Then they stood side by side unmoving for a long time, touching in silent communion, the heavy outline of the bull enclosing the more delicate line of the cow so that her form disappeared inside his.

Now the long twilight settles into soft stillness. The trees reveal their skeletons against the deepened sky. The first stars make mathematical statements of the essential nature of Elsewhere. And then the spaces inside these geometries gradually thicken with the twinkling tapestry of universal maya.

JULY 2

Up on the ridge above the coastline an old logging road runs through the forest. No humans dwell there. This afternoon I ventured off that road into the woods until I came to a quiet clearing. While I loitered there absorbing timelessness I began to see everything sharply: leaves, cobwebs, clouds, mosses. With crystalline vision I saw everything my feet touched: the beetles in the dirt, the grasses blowing in the wind, the clustering star flowers. Forms and colors jumped out in sharp suchness. The trees raised their arms in magnificent contours. Wherever I paused everything vibrated and it was I and I was it.

I saw the discarded, the blighted, the dying in the forest as part of the wonder, beautifully necessary to the new burgeoning. I became aware of the immense underness of the earth and now the wind moved over the roots, moving everything, keeping everything alive. I heard one old tree creak its bones as a woodpecker flew out of it. That was when I thought of Brahma, Vishnu, and Shiva in their busy trinity and of their jaunty "son" Krishna, that Orpheus Hermes Jesus boy. I saluted all my indwelling poet companions and all the gone lovers of my herohood.

I saw on a cedar log and played seesaw with it. Straddling that long thick log, I suddenly felt it to be a great penis, the largest in the world, and I laughed aloud, feeling that mine was equally large. Mine was the largest in the world, as well as the smallest in the world, there was no difference in these matters when everything came together. I felt I could aim that log like a phallic cannon at the far hillside and penetrate it all the way into the hot fire at the center of the earth.

At this point Horus the hawkgod circled above me, first as shadow, then as cry, then in the gliding power of his unity with the wind. I think I saw for the first time what a hawk is. As I saw a huckleberry lead. And a yellow wildflower. An old bottle of Outboard Motor Oil and a rusted hinge and a rotting stump.

What an hour it was, what an eternity. Everything was all right just as it was. Just as it is. Myself included.

JULY 3

I clambered on the cliff between two equal smells: the briny breath of the sea from below and the newly cut hay of the meadow above. I felt quite drunken with the sense of Yes, Yes of course, this is how it has always been: how simple the complexity, how complex the simplicity!

* * *

When I went to bed last night I experienced a surprising equilibrium. As I lay back on the pillow, I heard myself saying: Everything has always been here one way or another. So it must know what it's doing. And since I am part of this everything, a good part of me must be all right just the way it is, and the way it's doing.

And I said: I shall fulfill whatever I shall fulfill, however small or incomplete it may be. As long as I am true to my own gods and conscious of my vertical and my horizontal response-ability to them, how can I fear for my essential being?

Then I closed my eyes and I entered a family parlor and found my grandfather, after whom I am named, sitting there with his own father who was named Job. I thought you were dead, I said to old James R., sitting on a sofa waiting for his dinner. He looked at me appraisingly. He said, You think a lot of foolishness, don't you? And he turned to nod goodbye to my crippled aunt, who was going to a dance at the British Embassy dressed as Scheherazade.

JULY 4

In the vivid light of the calm afternoon I set off for a walk to the old cemetery of Cuffey's Cove. Along the road I spoke to the quail out with their children. I also spoke to a gopher snake.

This morning at breakfast Bill had been talking about communicating with animals: how Rin-Tin-Tin used to like having poetry read to him for fifteen minutes every day, how Ella Young coaxed a panther out of his cage by addressing him O Noble One, reveal yourself! and how Dorr Bothwell's father used to talk to the ants in San Diego and persuade them not to come into the house.

When I spoke to the snake on the path I questioned his antiquity. Have all animals resisted modernization and remained as they were in ancient times? Speaking to them shouldn't one address respectfully their primeval nature? Thus one might hope to learn some ageless instinctual wisdom. Even from the ill-tempered blackbirds along these roads.

I came to a small glen by the roadside where a stream trilled under moisty laurels. Thinking it would be pleasant to explore, I climbed the fence where a sign said No Trespassing Private Property of Nonella Bros, and I stepped down beside the creekbed. Here was a place more modest than the surrounding moors, cliffs, and redwoods. Here was a place for dryads to bathe. I sat listening to the voice of the stream.

Suddenly I heard behind me what I took to be a crowd of people. I turned to see a hefty snorting bull lumbering down the hillside at me. Behind him his creamy-colored wives stopped still in their tracks to stare. I took to my heels up the slippery hillside, hearing a man's voice shout, You better look for a tree! That bull is fierce!

The twig I first grabbed for wasn't there, my foot slipped from what rooting I counted on, my pulse banged. I didn't even consider standing my ground to speak to this creature. Ignominiously scratched and panting, I managed to climb out of the bull's range. Finally his magnificent thickness moved on, and the procession of his ladies followed. To the rancher in his jeep I shouted an apology for both my trespassing and my terror. He was not amused.

When they all had gone by, I started back to the fence and the road. But there I encountered Junior: a young bull bringing up the rear of the procession. Since he was even less pleased than his pa to see me and more eager to show off his aggressiveness, I had to make a second unseemly retreat. I scrambled over the fence completely out of breath, feeling I had trespassed not on the Nonella Bros but into the kingdom of the Bull God.

In order to see the Protestant graves at the cemetery I had to trespass again on Nonella Bros land, this time into a field separating the Catholics from the Presbyterians. There a black-faced ram defended his thick and woolly tribe. To reach the toppled gravestones of the Scottish settlers of the region I had to run the gauntlet of a Ram God. He was not pleased either and charged at me. His sheep ladies gamboled in circular disarray. Both the Bull and the Ram in one afternoon!

Despite neglect the graveyards seemed very recent compared to the domain of these animal kings. Has a ram's or a bull's nature changed much since sheep and cattle first appeared on the earth? How different were their thoughts or feelings when they traveled with Noah?

I also spoke today to a hermit thrust, a rabbit, and a rose worm. But I established the happiest communication with a gnat, who really did leave off hopping on my ear and flew out the window as I asked him to. A very odd Fourth of July.

* * *

Noontime was consecrated to the fruits of the sea. The water has been glassy for two days and the tides low. One of the guests at the inn came up from the cove with two splendid abalone he had pulled from a rock. He abhorred the taste of the creatures, so Bill and I removed them from their iridescent shells and feasted on them. Another guest came up, with four red snappers and a rock cod. The kitchen table looked like a Dutch still life. I was fascinated by the intense colors, the aquamarine eyes, the fins like prehistoric fans, the textures and hues of the innards. I questioned the brightest eye of the largest creature: O fish, tell me of the Sea! How did we all begin?

*   *   *

Now it is just before midnight. On the window opposite my writing table there are six different moths outstretched between the pane and the starry night beyond. Each is a fantastic design, the largest as boldly marked as a tiger.

I have practiced my guitar and I now can play Go Tell Aunt Rhody. I have a water tumbler filled with five different roses from the garden. I have looked at the latest archaeological photos from Ethiopia in the Illustrated London News and I have read in the Tao Te Ching: "Meandering leads to perfection, the crooked becomes straight, the empty full and the worn-out new." A spider is now walking on the inside of the windowpane, walking on the light-hypnotized forms of the moths. The sea sounds gentle tonight, there is an occasional bleat from the pasture, the moon will be very late.

JULY 5

It became a night of roses and horses. I took fullblown roses into my bed to anoint myself with petals. A bower of fragrance and soft touch to lie in. O Rosa Alba, skin as soft as that of the Shulamite!

I clutched her breasts, I caressed her nipples with petals, I kissed her corolla. Her pollen anointed my phallus. Ride, lovely rose, ride!

And I awoke to horses. Prancing black creatures galloped directly toward me on their way to being executed at dawn.

How could I rescue them from the firing squad? Before their own execution they had to haul away the dead bodies of other steeds. For this they were harnessed to a long sled. Smoke curled from their black nostrils, their executioners wore surgical masks. If I could free these horses, what tremendous energies I might unleash!

And today gave us a crystalline blaze of sun. These waters are not often so blue serene, so Greek, intimate enough to permit mermaids ashore or a shell for Venus to sail upon.

When I went down to the cove this afternoon, I sat as close to the Sea as I could, to watch and to listen. I saw the cormorants diving, I saw the sea palms waving their fronds, I uncovered a starfish with nineteen legs. I felt I could address a personal question: O Sea, how deep do things go?

In reply the Sea whooshed and whished. All she said, however, was: Yes...Yes...

JULY 6

The moth on the outside of the black windowpane is so frantic with a desire to reach the Impossible Light in my room that he grows more desperate by the moment. In the dark sky beyond, a single star flashes delicate signals. Do moths ever fly to the moon?

Last night the Rose came to me as a maiden Aphrodite of incomparable fragrance yearning for penetration and male sweat. What joy to caress her, to hold her breasts, to feel her velvet depths!

She had risen to me out of the limpid Greek sea of the afternoon and stepped easily ashore, knowing I had been waiting for what I did not expect. Her succulence, her ampleness delighted my Hermes.

Grateful have her in my bed I made love to her with princely tenderness. I was not only Hermes, I was Zeus disguised as a bull. In my phallus all the power of Zeus thundered. Where the Rose and the Fire were One burned a high mercurial union.

Now she rises in my breasts. They are formed of her roses. They mate with my Hermes. Come to me, my heart's hermaphrodite! Tell me who you are, tell me who we become, tell me what our love demands!

JULY 10

I believe everything in me is changing: my body, my thinking, my sexuality, my feelings, my view of the world. Does it show? Sometimes in the dining room I wonder if guests can behold in my face any telltale evidence of my secrets. But no one looks twice, no one wants to see. They are preoccupied with their own fantasies or with being unpleasant to one another.

Why do men betray one another, plot against one another, ill one another? Why do they kill rather than embrace? Wouldn't they enjoy loving one another? I suppose not. Men fear joy too much, fear their instincts. Fear a surrender to their feelings. Fear loving themselves in others and loving others in themselves. Fear loving their true gods. Fear loving their own androgynes.

Have men always been terrified of their true nature? Is all history a record of their denials of themselves?

JULY 12

Visitors seldom climb down to the cove. Today I went there with an offering of flowers and I stood for a long time in the chill water. As I tossed each flower into the waves, I invoked the compassion of the Sea:

O unchanging custodian of everchanging depths and surfaces, hear me, mighty mother, listen to my heart.

Where I stand in your waves you are cool, elsewhere your currents flow warm. Here you rock gentle and calm, elsewhere you rage violent and destructive.

You encompass your opposites, you circulate your identity, you polarize your dominions.

From sunken treasure to limpid rock-pool you contain all residues and renewals.

From your depths you hold up the continents like offerings to the sky.

O share with me your potencies. Do not let me drown in my swamp. Do not let my inner gales shipwreck me.

Teach me to yield to the storms that toss me. Teach me to float on my fears.

Let me ebb and flow in my own dance of time. Let me drum and lilt and roar like you. Let me permeate, absorb, endure!

* * *

When I returned to my cabin I practiced Blow Ye Winds on my guitar and was distracted by the hummingbird fuchsias outside my window.

JULY 13

An intangible sadness wells up in me at the dinner hour, like the grieving of an exile. And I feel I am back in the house of Mrs. Rhino. But despite my loneliness among the guests I hold onto the promise of an equilibrium yet to be found. And what can be the offspring of hermaphroditic wedding? What creature, what creation, what destiny?

* * *

In the art class I am in theory astute but in practice a duncehead. Today I kept mixing the green for moss when I wanted the green for seaweed. Where does my true skill lie? What felicity can be salvaged from my murky depths? Could this emerging Androgyne be the poet whom I have always honored but did not believe existed?

I went again to the Sea today, I brought her flowers. Her wave rolled toward me like an answering embrace and broke over my ankles. She is still saying Yes...

* * *

In the night the wind blew, but the cypresses did not move. A strange man came into my room and got in bed with me. He had brought me a Tinker Toy. He said he was Irwin my father.

He certainly was heavier than I.

Where have you been all these years? I asked. I've been waiting so long for you, and now it is too late.

You are my son, he answered. You should know how deep my heart lies buried. I had a sweet friend who was all my joy. And he had a soul bride we both had to marry.

Then my father hugged me. He encircled me with his grizzly strength and filled me with honey. He hugged me til he wept.

I woke up weeping too. That's what I thought. Actually I was drenched in sweat.

I didn't get the chance to ask my father what I have always wanted to know: did he die of pneumonia because his beloved friend had been killed in action in France? Or because my mother emasculated him?

I didn't get the chance to tell him how, the year after he died, Olga had taken me to the hospital to have "my tonsils removed" and I woke up with my penis cut off. Or so I thought. For there was a bandage all around it and it hurt. No one had warned me that I was to be circumcised.

JULY 14

Quietly in the forest on the ridge the sunlight lay in golden pools among the trees. I felt like a latecomer interrupting an eternal concert of silence.

I sat down to listen. But then, damn! I felt a stirring in my bowels. Would I have to go back to the village to shit? Why should I? Why not defecate right here in this grove?

I sat on my heels like the peasant in Torremolinos who squatted every day across the road from our rented villa. When I turned to look at what I had done I saw a finely shaped turd fallen in a long spiral. It had a blunt nose and tapered to a pointed tail at the end. The significance of my shit struck me: here in this grassy circle I had made an offering to the Earth Mother out of my own body in an utterly natural way. I was as amazed as a child by the mystery of creating excrement.

In my awe I knelt to praise the wonders of earthly

processes, and to give thanks to the powers of this place. Beside my knee in the path lay a deer's black turd. A yellow rain of pollen floated through the sunlight. A blue jay cackled from a branch. I felt in holy vibration to things around me: gold and black butterflies, dragonflies in sport, little gray birds who whistled like squirrels. I responded to every tremor, to the sounds of going and growing, to the quivering silence. High over the treetops hawks circled.

*   *   *

On the road back as I passed an abandoned farm, I saw a colony of black vultures perched along the fence where a young doe lay dead, her throat but by barbed wire. Beyond on a bleached tree sat three ravens. A jackrabbit ran across the road from one side, a chipmunk from the other.

I stopped by another grove. There I undressed, and was naked as when Man began, feeling the Sun God warming and blessing my flesh and hair, feeling my life fly upward in gratitude.

JULY 15

The hairs on my chest are turning to gold. Alchemy of the Sun God! I look upon myself as a new creature. To have soft golden hair shining from my own body is like having the beauty of my First Beloved to wear, like having his flesh enrobe my own. Thanks to the stranger who left a bottle of hydrogen peroxide in the medicine cabinet Father Sun is giving me my own Golden Fleece. It shimmers over the breasts of my Aphrodite.

Her flowering I can touch her in my nipples, can grasp with heroic passion, can lie with in hot delight. Touching her left breast in mine, I am at the hearth of my heartbeat. She adores the blaze of my Hermes. She loves the sunburst of his penis and his male milk that feeds the bride and sustains the goddess.

What generates the intense love affair of my innermost He and She? Is it a self-loving initiation that lives through me? An ancient mystery of the cells as much as of the gods? Has it inspired all quests for inner unity since Adam was first divided?

* * *

This morning I took a newly-opened morning glory to the Sea and placed it on her shoulder where she rested upon the rocks of low tide, her kelp-plaited hair undulating as she dozed. I knelt beside her as worshipful lover who knows he will never possess his adored one but humbly brings her a tribute from the element on which he dwells. I will write her a love song. I will give it to her to absorb in her own way.

I wish I could give the Sea as personal an offering as I gave the Earth yesterday. Perhaps some of my hair, from my chest or my pubis. Or a fingernail. I can now understand that imperiled mariner who in order to appease a typhoon cut off his finger and threw it overboard.

* * *

This afternoon the cove lay hot and clear. I tried to paint a literal watercolor of the beach. But I could not resist placing a unicorn in it.

I have long cherished the unicorn because his spiraling phallic emblem springs from his third eye, and points toward heaven. With his indestructible delicacy, his lunar mantle and his solitariness, he is the fabled symbol for the enlightened hermaphrodite, for the elegant instinct of the Spirit, for the savior who comes from we know not where and returns thither.

JULY 16

Apollo embrace me today! Sometimes I find myself so ecstatic with these secrets that it is hard not to blurt them to Bill or to any congenial-looking stranger. But I dare confide only in the Sea or my journal or the spider on the windowpane. Who else would believe me?

It happened this afternoon, in that special meadow in the woods where I seek the sunlight out of the sea wind. And how surprising, for Apollo has never been intimate or immediate to me. Yet today he emerged from the Sun in benevolent and harmonic majesty. And I extolled him thus:

Great Apollo, maestro of great sounds and silences, Meistersinger of melodies and language, your splendors have ignited my snows.

Let me now burn with your bounty, let your golden fire consume me. Let my energies dance, my spirit fly!

Golden my being at all its centers. Gild my genitals, gild my guts. Grant me a golden heart, a golden throat, a golden voice, a golden eye, a golden mind!

As I stood naked there in the heat I heard voices from the trees that encircled me, as if the sacred Nine were singing in unison from the branches. With eyes closed I raised my arms aloft and lifted my face to the Sun.

His warming caresses poured over me and enwrapped me. I could feel them prod and delineate me. I could feel them reach into the meridians of my body, ripple into nerves and organs. I could feel molten fingers forging the shape of my phallus. I could feel hot arrows pierce the root of my spine, warm my cold serpent there till it uncoiled and glided up the tree of my body, impregnating from within the whole of my Yggdrasil. O, to feel the sun-loving Serpent climb my spinal tree and transmute his solar power into energy and act.

Alleluia to you, Apollo of the golden hair. Lead me back to my primal Golden Age. Lead me forward to my own Apollenation. Teach me how to glow and radiate my life!

JULY 19

Shame is no longer relevant. For the god grows in my genitals now, blesses my whole body, animates all its centers. I feel high reverence and wonder, I could go as naked as a dog or a bull. For my sex is part of the divine whole, is beautiful as the stars, is the chaos and glory of Eros.

When I took flowers to the cove this evening I recognized the sea as fellow androgyne. I felt thrust and bellow blending with shudder and ripple. I grinned to acknowledge Poseidon but gave my tribute to Amphitrite. This time the flowers I brought had witnessed my secret unions with the Rose.

From all those I offered her the Sea chose the tiger lily and pulled it into her body. My heart jumped. She had taken into herself the orange-bursting animal emblem, the flower most like the sun.

Like Samson's, my strength shines now in my hair. Wearing the cloak of light that the Sun has given me, I enter a new realm of knowing. This realm has no frivolous air, this is a solemn place that calls for the shedding of the trivial and the wasteful. Here one is expected to endure, to be both warrior and peacebringer, to be lover and savior and poet and friend. Here one is to be dedicated to the service of enlightening.

Is this my initiation so long postponed? Is this the apotheosis so painfully sought? For I stepped out of my old flesh, and all the distaste that encrusted it. I stepped forth shorn the bandages of my disgrace. I shed the skin of the unloved child and revealed a man to admire, blessed by the gods of light.

This benediction I have repeatedly asked of my gurus. But I had to give it to myself. This shining new fellow is the offspring of my sacred mating, when the rose of the Sea and the lion of the Fire became One.

My genitals no longer belong to me. They serve the Sun in its redemption of the Moon. Behind me on the road through the wasteland lies the corpse of an imprisoned child.

JULY 21

In this unfamiliar region Sun and Moon and Sea and Earth become more meaningful to me than human beings. Is this the realm beyond the opposites, beyond the delusions of the mortal coil? Is this the Nirvanic threshold?

Most of the amusements that sustain life's activity for everybody else begin to seem meaningless, especially the world of competitiveness, proof and acquisition. What stirs me most fully each day now: my devotion to the gods and to the God that includes them all. Whenever I am prevented from my communion with them I sour and bristle.

I go every day to the Sea with veneration and praise. This morning very early I took her a newly picked rose. It was a token offering of the rose I carry in my breast. To accompany it I plucked a golden hair from my chest. I never fail to receive some grace from the Sea. For the first time in my life I am on joyful terms with her.

So am I also with the Sun. Each afternoon returning from Mendocino I hasten to encounter him in the forest. My genitals quicken with anticipation at the very thought of being able to enter the woods and there accept a hot golding embrace. It has become the holiest moment of my days, and the most ecstatic.

I remove my clothes, I kneel, I remain for a long time inventing orisons, offering my being to the world's most radiant source. I feel his touch grow warmer, gilding the grasses of my flesh into an ever more dazzling robe. I feel my phallus partake of his sublime energy. I open my moth to let his gold nectar pour in the top of my head bursts into a sweat of song.

Light and Heat of the Heavens, how powerfully your hands dispel my leadenness! Your have shown me how to give myself the warmth of new vision, you have revealed to me how I can adore you in myself. What offerings dare I bring to you? I can understand Aztecs and Mayans. Nothing seems adequate now short of a human sacrifice. In acknowledgment of this I offer my own life to your service.

Dare I sing to you? O Apollo, could you teach me the secret of music?

* * *

Last night I saw Artemis at half-moon glowing over the sea, the stars her necklaces, the water reflecting her silver hair. Despite the wind I disrobed and knelt naked on my little porch in full view of her. I asked her quicksilver forces to companion my golden ones. She smiled, she has had to listen to me for years. From her benevolence have come baskets of dream, the Eros mystery, the veils of Annie, the fitful incandescence. Last night she smiled and kissed me. Again I felt the union of Sea and Moon within me.

* * *

I could not go to art school today. I had to be about my Lord's business: clearing the pollen path to redemption. In Apollo's company I discover the fellowship of Hermes with his lyre, Pan with his pipes, Krishna with his flute, those who sing of the finite infinite and the immortal mortalities. To assert, to assert. To mate Eros to Logos. To sing the divine unions!

Was it Apollo who performed the ceremony that married my Hermes to my Aphrodite? Since he enlightens every opposite, is he himself the brightest androgyne of all? Does he call me to his brotherhood?

O Lord of Song, make me worthy! Teach me your exercises and excesses! Ignite my sluggish waters, enflame my mountains! I could ask nothing greater than to be a singing servant of the ultimate secrets of clarity. Can I do justice to the dominance of the Sun in my trines? Dare I dream of the company of David, of Dante, of Blake?

I shall lapse, I shall fall, it is the measure of my clay. But I shall not forget my oath. I will endure whatever my failing, for I know this much of the law: that all living things are meant to fulfill their natures fully, and to help this to happen is our human task.

I await my orders.

I have been for hours at my secret place in the forest worshipping the Sun. His laying-on of hands provides that supreme tactility, which I have been seeking throughout my years: the touch of God himself. It limbers the muscles of the soul. It dries out my dim marshes and murky ponds. It warms the fluids inside me so that they flow from chakra to chakra, oiling the path of my Kundalini.

I trust the incandescence of my divine Arsonist. Each day he ripens my goldening more, like a confirmation of his severe love.

I sang aloud in the forest.

JULY 22

O the overpowering joy! Last night a more riotous and profounder experience of the sacred marriage.

After my hymn to the midnight moon in the windy night, I lay sweaty on my bed. I could feel the enticing Venus within me, she who is the consort of my kingdom. I could make love to her visible bloom till she squirmed and stretched in delight. Then I could be She, the queen loving the king in me, strong-legged He, lithe, hot from the heat of the Sun. With her I could make subtle love to his manhood till it ripened and towered in desire. Finally the royal pair met in mutual adoring play, breast and phallus in equally passionate caress, souls separate and together at the same time.

But then, as their ecstatic conjunction heightened, I paused. I realized this was not meant for their personal pleasure nor for mine. I realized this must be a sacrifice. A holy act was being performed, a play of the eternal opposites begun in Eden.

So I lit a candle and held it under my phallus until it burned the flesh.

Then I knelt in ardent homage as my King Hermes and Queen Aphrodite enacted the culmination of their life-giving ecstasy for the wholeness of my Androgyne. It was for Him for Him, my own Apollo, my Rebis,* my Father Bride!

And as the love liquid of the sacred union spilled forth sputtering the candle I felt it like a tidal wave of tears, like a weeping of joy for a wonder greater than my life.

*　　*　　*

This ecstasy of flesh and soul overwhelms me. This reality of the One who is the Two in One is my Hermaphrodeity.

The power of such flowering converts my body into a mating ground for all opposites in heat. It unites me to the ram jumping the ewe in the field, to the hummingbirds swooping together in the air, to the self-fertilizing fruit tree, to Adam giving birth to Eve, to Plato's Beloved, to Shiva dancing with his Shakti.

How can one sing of this dazzle? How crazy must I be to find words for exhilaration? Why not wed the earthy to the sublime, the cuckoo to the cosmic, the erotic to the sacred?

Tis something to remember. That ecstatic revels are a necessity of nature. That Jesus should have danced. That clowns are necessary to make Prospero's magic shine. That maenads caroused for Dionysus. That Helen eloped with Paris. And Krishna flirted and fucked and tricked and fluted.

Well, so be it and so let it become, if so it will. And if so, I shall happily be god's sobering numbskull.

JULY 23

Can you accept yourself, in every part and particular? Specifically, tenderly and humbly? Can you learn to love yourself with gusto?

Each day I relish my sunblest body more, love my breasts as sensuous and my penis as formidable, and their uniting in me

*(Editor's note: This refers to a passage from a book called *The Androgyne: Reconciliation of Male and Female* by Elemire Zolla:

Hermes Trismegistus, the legendary founder of alchemy, points to the primal mystery in nature, the principle of fire, which enfolds in its fourfold flames the two essential opposites, sun and moon, male and female, sulphur and mercury, which become the one androgyne at all moments of conception and birth in nature...

The process is threefold. It starts with a first, embryonic androgyne phase which in the case of mineral bodies takes place when in the bowels of the earth a nitrous, salty soil is impregnated with an acrid, corrosive vapour; the two are gathered together by the principles of sunlight which enter the earth in the form of dew. The same dew that nourishes the life of plants can also activate this volatility beneath the earth. The result is called primal matter, or Rebis, or fiery androgyne (both principles being acrid and burning), or Adam (because they are the first engendering principle in the mineral world).)

as heavenly wonder. And yet I begin to feel something of me not yet brought to light. I have the sense of a painful vulnerability I cannot locate. Is it behind me in some neglected place? What lurks in my shadow that the Sun does not reach?

This is something my guardians should know. Yesterday in the forest they urged me to leave another offering from my bowels. I scarcely expected then to see my serpentine turd being devoured by a large worm. It made me aware of how much the Earth Mother wants such offerings. If one does not dedicate them to her, does she exact revenge?

*   *   *

In my dream I saw Annie in a smock teaching students to plunge their hands into muck and shape a grail out of it. The class emerged from her room with mudpie fingers and symbolic shit on their aprons. Mix the colors, Annie said, from the earth reds, from the orange fireball, and do something monumental with them.

Last night I did her bidding my own way. Was it connected with the pain I had felt while washing my anus in the shower before dinner? I had been asking then, why do I continue to have this hypersensitive ass that is as prudish and pinched as a Puritan maid?

I mixed the colors and began to paint. Made from the yellow and orange of the sun and the green of the glowing earth, the colors darkened to reddish brown. Shapes growing out of the colors became slippery creatures of mouse and worm life in fecal browns crawling around a yellow-green marshland. I gave each creature a bright lapis eye.

I thought the picture shitty enough when I finished it and went to bed. When I looked this morning at the glass of water where all the brushes had soaked, it was the actual color of the turd I had left in the forest.

When two opposite colors are fully blended, the result is the color of shit. When sun gold and sea blue meet as equals they become shit. When all colors are blended the result is the color of shit. Is this what the spectrum of solar light boils down to? Is the color of Oneness, then, the color of shit?

* * *

This morning as I sat at my window warming my pelvis in the Sun, I began to wonder what about my dark underside?

I turned around and bent over. I tried to open up my tight asshole to the Sun that he might warm it, melt it, heal it. I begged him to shed light deep into this cave that I might feel some love for its malodorous function.

Just then I saw a brown field mouse outside my window nibbling a nasturtium. He could have climbed out of my yesterday painting. I realized he must be one of the creatures whose rumbles and skitters I hear in the walls at night. He belongs to my company of shadows, as do also the crawlies I painted.

At this point my bowels began to heave. Feeling I had to bring this to the attention of the gods, I fetched my palette plate from last night and I defecated into the middle of it.

Then I held the plate up to the light, smelt, examined, praised it: here out of my own guts I had made this golden-brown serpent. Before I surrendered it to the toilet I raised it up to the Sun as an offering:

My Lord Sun, teach me how to accept what I was taught to reject. Show me the beauty of fetor and slop. Thanks to you I take joy in my genitals. Can I find the same delight with my anus? Can I enjoy its comings and goings? Can I permit it to be penetrated?

* * *

Bill and I are just back from a trip up Greenwood Creek: a clear vocal stream, troutfilled, polliwogged, skater-bugged. When Bill went off to gather mosses, I removed my clothes and stood in the water listening to its voices. This is the first time here that I have been intimate with a river. From it I learned things the Sea did not know. Strongest was a vision of this stream being my own alimentary canal, its final exit the so-called mouth of the river. I saw it as my labyrinthine inner world, the gurgling kingdom of my natural fluidity, the home of the yielding Yin always seeking the lowest level. I saw my inner riverbed from my esophagus to my anus as the route of my uroboric reality.

I wish I had the courage to eat my own shit. It would be a ritual act to acknowledge the end as a beginning. (I looked up feces: it progresses from feculent to fecund. Fecit, the old masters signed their paintings.)

Shitting is a wonder to be honored. Not only its outcomes but the internal alembic where the alchemical process occurs. Blighted in childhood, that place of inner fire has caused me stomach ache, vomit or diarrhea ever since.

Rightly isn't this the home of a metamorphic power? Isn't this a natural dwelling place for a deity?

JULY 24

Last night I made love to her in her secret place. She is the Annie of my unknown waterworks, she is the fierce virgin, she is the keeper of my serpents.

I found her pulsating, delicate, and horrified. I caressed the mouth of her river cave. I tried gently to penetrate her. What had been my pain for years transformed slowly into energetic pleasure. I felt her unfold with gratitude, with a surging zest that comes only after the end of grief. A deep trembling resounded through me. It came close to hurting, as great joy can. As love does.

Today I think how terribly she has been abused, how she bled with her wounds, how she closed up and wept. Bravely she has endured. I would like to honor her with special tenderness.

Shouldn't one consider more carefully what offerings one brings to nourish her, instead of dumping any old debris into her river? For the body is temple of the holiest of holies, contains all complementary powers of time and eternity. Man, if he but knew himself, is the most sacred edifice on earth. For he contains all his gods and goddesses, with all their conflicting powers.

* * *

This evening the air was mist-thick, the tide higher than I have ever seen it. The Sea became a hidden lake in that foggy dark. I had brought a pink rose from my bedroom. She slashed it with her wave, tore off the petals, flung the stem back at my feet.

Wind woke me in the night, I thought, shaking the cabin and banging the trees. My papers whirled around the room. I got up to shut the window. But a sea captain stood before me, barring my way.

Don't try to stop the wind, he shouted.

Why not? I asked.

What do you think turns the world? What fans the flames, makes the waves, carries the seeds, shapes the years? Let it blow through you. Let it blow you away.

He puffed his cheeks and blew at me.

You look like my father, I said.

I thought he smiled at me then.

JULY 25
Feast of St. James

After my first probing in the cave of my river goddess, I felt a new spaciousness opening my pelvis. And I went to sleep flooded with wonder, feeling farther inside myself than I had ever expected to penetrate. It was like reaching a place where pain marries pleasure and discovers unsuspected harmony.

This morning, driving through the fog to Mendocino, I was evaluating the treasure of this goddess. Suddenly the reply came: das Rheingold. Isn't she the gold guarded by the Rhine Maidens, the gold within, the gold at the bottom of the river, the precious immortality to be sought in the bowels of the earth?

Later in the day I went down to the Sea with a newly plucked rose. I took it to the small cave at the end of the beach, which I have claimed as a private shrine for my intestinal goddess. In the salty wet cave multi-colored seaweeds lay upon russet pebbles. I placed the flower there on a long black stone. And I prayed to her:

O dark, autonomous Lady allow me to know your inner mystery. Open for me the door of your cave. Let me enter, despite my terror!

This brought me to sobbing. Was this like that first afternoon I sat upon the beach, when I searched for my identity among the stones? Now I was searching for another part of myself. I put my hand into this seacave as I had tried last night to reach into the rivercave of my newly discovered mistress.

Desiring again to be closer to the earth I stretched out face down upon the pebbles. From that angle I looked sidewise at the Sea, looked deep into her pulsing body. Her white foam became a handkerchief rushing up the shore to meet my tears.

Then I remembered my patron saint and my eager pilgrimage to his shrine at Compostela. I imagined St. James the fisherman in a cove like this one being interrupted by Jesus: Lay down your net and follow me, we shall be fishers of men.

The legend tells that James, wearing his pilgrim hat and his scallop shell, carrying his book and his hermetic staff, traveled in a stone boat to Spain to rescue the shackled land of Iberia from the Moors. He was willing to make his life a valiant pilgrimage, for he had known God in man and he had been loved by his redeemer. So he is patron saint of Spain, and also of alchemists and all cosmological artists.

I have no stone boat, only a blood colored stone. But I would relish a spiritual quest. Shall I ever be admitted to such a brotherhood as the Order of the Golden Hair? Might another great androgyne like Jesus stop me by the sea one day and call me forth to serve the redemption of mankind?

JULY 26

O shy dark one, allow love to enter your valleys, your rivulets and lakes, and thus to flow forth like the Rhine itself, like all rivers of time. Within your veiled portal deep wonders dwell, mysterious spaces, liquid rhythms, luscious warmth.

Today when I went to my sacred grove to visit the Sun Father, I exposed my rear to him that he might reach into her cave. I besought him to irradiate her river mouth into a benevolent delta, to treat her to the golden thrust of Apollo's love, to woo her into the wholeness of life. If I could anoint her mouth with the elixir of Hermes, would she wish to mate with him?

Knowing at last where she dwells I want to do her honor, I want to savor every part of her, I want her to know how she belongs to me. With her many tributaries she is the dancer of my processes: nerves, blood, semen, breath. She is more than Rhine Maiden, she is as powerful as Kali, she is shadow mate of the great Sun who shone in upon her today.

Does this bring me closer to the source of my old woes? Isn't it in her region that I have had chronic suffering since childhood when there was so much she could not stomach? Yet I had faith that ultimately she could digest anything. Meanwhile behind my back she gobbled my nourishing energies.

Feeling the Sun penetrate her now so stimulated me that I had suddenly to shit. I went to my special dell nearby, where my previous offerings had disappeared without a trace.

This time I was acutely conscious of my turd coming down the Amazon within me. Like a godly giant, I deposited my flowing land mass upon the Earth Mother and left it steaming there.

JULY 29

I was watching the people ahead of me in line for the Fort Bragg bus. Though their eyes were open, were they seeing anything? They seemed to be locked behind built-in notions and no-nos, unaware of the mystery living through them or of the dance of illusion surrounding them.

Don't they need a voice to call them out of their blind alleys? Don't they need a poet who will grasp them by the heart? Don't they need the ears of their souls tweaked with music of the gods? Otherwise they will remain moths banging against the window, ants on ant highways, creatures of herd and hive.

A poet needs to recognize the divine essence of his fellow mortals, however disorderly or dull they may appear. He needs to have the courage of his own illuminations. He needs to be as willing as Abraham to sacrifice his only begotten son. Otherwise he remains merely a literary person.

I can address a lizard or a bull with respect for its essence. Why not a man as well? How do you look upon other men as astonishing organisms? Only by so regarding yourself.

Love love love, with awe and delight, the facts and functions. As I become loving toward my bodily organs where formerly I fretted them, I begin to feel new hereness. My He and She shine brighter together.

O to heal, to awaken, to redeem! To be a voice, not a literary man. Yes. For I am in love with the eternities of things, I am in love with metamorphoses.

JULY 30

Gloriously, my ancient virgin bride, O yes, my two way wonder! Be fed at both ends, my darling. Let things come and go in their beautiful give and take.

Were we not united last night in the most rapturous of unions? I love you, I live you, I wing with the knowing that you are in me and with me, that I can enter you and feel you at any time.

I dreamt of Irwin, my own human father. He was making a pair of wings, shaping their transparencies in iridescent tints. Were they for some monumental butterfly?

Then I realized they were my size. He was preparing this miraculous winged mechanism for me, that I should be an Icarus who would not fail and fall. By this patient attention of his, might I journey where no other son has ever been?

* * *

This morning before breakfast I went down to the cove at very low tide. I have never seen the Big She so relaxed. She lay blissful upon her couch, her hair down, her robes and ornaments sprawled carelessly in the disarray of erotic fulfillment. Offshore the rippling currents quivered like flesh remembering rapture.

Standing at the entrance to the arched tunnel through the cliff I watched the tides flowing in and then out, forward and back, perpetually renewing their light and color with the breathing of the ocean. It seemed the most natural paradox in the world.

JULY 31

My experiences these last two days have been shattering. Only now, close to midnight on the very last day of this fateful July, am I compelling myself to try to write it down. I am still shaken. My legs quiver when I think of what happened.

It began yesterday afternoon. Uneasy with some strange longing in the foggy light, I felt I had to leave the chatter of gossip and opinion after lunch. Thinking I wanted sunlight, I sought my special clearing in the forest. But it was foggy on the ridge as well. Lacily foggy, veiling the highest treetops, clothing the woods in moist quiet. The only sound was an intermittent drip drip from the leaves.

Quietly and cautiously I entered the tree-encircled dell where on three different days I had made my worm-colored offerings to the Earth Mother. The third turd I had left only a few days ago. That one too had completely disappeared.

It was at that moment that I became aware of how intricately I had become involved in a solemn ceremony in this hallowed place. Three times here the Mother of All Things had taken into herself my innermost offerings, the snakes from my bowels.

Embracing a tree I cried out: She accepts me! At last I

am accepted as one of her own! Once I began to love what I disliked and to love her within it, she accepts she accepts! I am no longer alien and unwanted!

I fell to my knees praising her, and praising the mystery of compassion. It seemed some miracle of light had passed into me.

Thank you, Father Sun, for taking me into your care. Here in this place I could know you and the Mother most nakedly. Now she too has blessed me.

But the initiations were not yet ended. This special grove had become a temenos of the Great Goddess where the surrounding ring of trees stood as her attendant witnesses. Gazing upon that circle of moist leaf-covered earth, which I had visited on many afternoons, I beheld it now as if it were the actual breathing flesh of She, the Most Adored One.

How can I unite my life with yours? I said aloud. How can I feel you more deeply a part of me?

To my surprise my penis had stiffened with desire. And then came the irrational impulse for what seemed suddenly the only inevitable act. Where I felt she lay most amply in the center of that circle, there with reverence and amazement I dropped my hand to the ground and began tenderly to reach into her. Under the stiff leaves and pine needles her soil was ashy, surprisingly soft and inviting. I knew I had to reach deeply, had to be more completely one with her. It was for this task that the Sea and the Sun had been preparing me. And it had to be an act of love.

I dug the hole deep. Then I thrust my penis in, not without a flash of fear that I might be committing a desecration. She was harsh, she was painfully real, she was magnificent. I plunged as far into her as I could, my chest leaning down upon her ferns, my hands reaching out upon her whole continent. I felt like some sacrificial hero of antiquity I remembered mythologies of Sky Father cohabiting with Earth Mother to create the world.

Such a scary ecstasy shook me. I yelled out, We are One, we are One!

A squawking jay flew up overhead. My seed lay deep in the earth.

*   *   *

When I withdrew my penis it was stained with her soft dirt. I pulled myself to my knees, feeling exhausted, exhilarated, and grateful. I felt I had initiated an alliance with Immortality.

As I thanked and praised her I covered her fertile hole with a cluster of pine needles. I also thanked the murmuring trees that attended us. I pocketed a leaf for a token. As if tiptoeing from the chamber where my Beloved slept, I withdrew to the road as quietly as I could.

At the entrance to this special place I noticed how the old logs fallen there had provided a natural enclosure for my secret marriage. Somehow this, like everything else, became awesomely significant. I was panting, drained, my eyes wet. I felt as if I had come to the top of some mountain I never expected to climb.

After so many despairing years of never being united to anything, suddenly I had become one very definite I: a Man united with the Her of everything, a Self connecting the powers of earth and heaven. I have won! I cried. And I am One! I have won! I have One!

As the tears rolled down my face and I stood upon the empty road that wound away through the fog, I began to feel terribly cold. Was it some intuition that my life would never be the same again? That I would now have to live up to some more chilling challenge?

*   *   *

Last night it was difficult to sleep. I kept hearing distant sounds of major upheavals: a war, a mass migration, a new ordering of faith? At dawn the wind moaned and wracked the trees.

All day today, with this experience reverberating through me, I felt oddly unreal. I wondered if I looked peculiar to everyone. But there was not a soul I could confide in. I made a mess of my guitar lesson.

This afternoon without intending it I was drawn again to the woods. I thought perhaps I might take some flowers there, or in any case check whether my experience had actually occurred. I was certainly not prepared for what happened.

I came cautiously into my grove. I looked down at the Earth where she lay, where I had lain with her. I looked at the passage I had made into her, where I had deposited my seed and where I had said a prayer for all the fruits that She and I might reap from our union.

All was as I had left it, the pubic pine needles concealing her cave. However, in front of it stretched a fat shit-colored gastropod worm, slowly advancing with tentacles extended. I had arrived at precisely the moment when this great worm was passing in front of the entrance that I had made into the Great Mother.

I remembered that my shit was the living talisman that had first brought me to this grove, and to this elemental bed of love. Here now this worm's shape was similar to the turd I had left in this place a few days ago: a blunt nose tapering to a long pointed tail. No wonder my spine shivered. In awe I fell to my knees.

This living turd-creature hypnotized me. I watched it slowly turn in my direction. I stared at it until I no longer found it repulsive. Strangely enough its fecal color resembled certain kelps of the sea. I was also fascinated by the way its tentacles pumped in and out as it swept oozily in my direction.

Three similar slugs loitered nearby. But this one coming toward me was much the largest, the queen of them perhaps. Was it she who had eaten my three turds?

Glistening, moisty, undulant, squishing her way over the fallen leaves, she advanced unswervingly toward my right knee. Her size was purely relative. I felt her to be as large and powerful as the Nonella bull. Plainly this was an encounter with a goddess, and this time the goddess was coming directly to me. Wasn't this the Worm Queen herself? And what did she want of me now?

Terror-struck, I feared that her touch might kill me on the spot. But I did not dare to draw back or even to move out of her path. However much I was shaking, I knew it was essential to hold my ground. When she did reach my knee, she halted just a hair's breadth before touching it.

Though I was in a cold sweat, I managed to speak to her. With cautious respect I praised her eminence, her special realm, her ancient right to be there. In response she turned aside and climbed upon a fungus where she curled into a loop as if to swallow her tail.

I was tempted to make the sign of the cross. I had been visited by an original chthonic It. I had been confronted by the Goddess of Life and Death herself, moving with the unhurried dignity of a dowager empress in heavy trailing robes. And in the color of my own shit.

AUGUST 1
Lammas

This morning's marvel: the turd I made in my toilet bowl was exactly the same size and shape and color as the Worm Queen herself. These symbols become unnervingly intimate.

Yet I recognized this as another stage in the enlightenment, which I had, without knowing it, come to this place to confront. This queen of the netherworld has been dwelling inside my body all my life. When finally I recognized this, then she revealed herself to me in the guise of shit walking.

It says in Bill's nature book that such worms "feed on decaying organic matter." Is it she who will be my ultimate devourer? Yesterday she was testing me. She saluted my presence, acknowledged my courage in not flinching, approved my recognition of her majesty. Then she passed by. That was as intimidating as a papal audience.

But now she had come out of me in effigy and occupied my toilet bowl. Before performing the indignity of flushing her away, I left her there while I shaved so that I could glance at her repeatedly and contemplate her meanings. Now she was telling me that if I had not made the effort to accept my own shit, I would never had encountered her or known her secret. And she was telling me that my fear of touching her was similar to my fear of touching my own shit. For hadn't my shit always fed the Worm Queen? And now couldn't I see here in my own toilet that I had also eaten her?

I realized during the day that this is only one of her many forms. Isn't she also the Rose whom I have bedded and the Aphrodite in my breast and the Goddess of the grove and the Artemis of the night and the Big She of the ocean? The Worm Queen, however, is her most disturbing manifestation: the Great Intestine we all inhabit. Hers is the kingdom where decay is the stuff of life.

I walk about dazed between Hosanna and Kyrie.

*   *   *

I sought solace of the Sea this afternoon. She was the one who first hinted of the secrets I would learn while living in this place. Today she came toward me, gracefully accepted my flowers, lay translucent at my feet. First I knelt on the pebbled shore, then I spread out face down upon the beach and looked across to her, as if she lay in a bed beside me.

I thanked her for the initiations that had begun for me in this cove. And I asked her once more to instruct me in the deep rhythms of profoundness that contain all the seeds of life. Her response was to make me feel that I was lying again upon the transformed flesh of the Goddess. This time her stony shore had become her breathing flesh. I began to caress her stones. I licked them. I stretched toward her, tingling with desire. I kissed her, I enclosed her, I melted her. I was boy, man, and Old One all at once. And I was wed to girl, woman, and Old Mother for all time.

AUGUST 2

Today I have been here forty days and forty nights. May this be the reason I begin to believe that this ordeal in the wilderness has nearly run its course? I know that I am depleted from being flung about among these transcendencies. Right now I am relieved to have the actuality of my guitar to hold. I can play On Top of Old Smokey without a mistake.

* * *

I have just been again to the sacred place. There yet another mystery awaited me. I had gone to the ridge seeking only warmth and radiance. But fog was blowing through my grove.

It felt eerie reentering that circle. The place seemed to quiver with invisible presences. A chill overtook me. I was almost afraid to look at the ritual marriage bed. When I came opposite it, I was stopped still. There right in the vagina I had opened, there where my penis had entered the earth, stretched the Worm Queen.

She seemed utterly at home. Had she just emerged from the hole? Had she taken up residence in it? Had she consumed my semen? As before, her three sisters lingered among the leaves nearby. I couldn't help believing that these smaller slugs were three of my turds transformed into living creatures.

Solemnly I saluted her. Rousing herself slowly, she began to move toward me at her implacable pace. I presented the offerings I had brought: the abundant yellow rose that has been in my room since the day I last came to the forest, a ripe nectarine, and a shiny black phallic stone that I found on the beach two days ago.

This stone I set some distance in front of me, pointing it lengthwise toward the hole. The petals of the rose I scattered. The fruit I pierced and set on either side of the stone.

Meanwhile the unhesitant Worm Queen advanced. First she came upon the phallic stone. To my astonishment I thought I saw her put her mouth over the end of it and swallow it whole. Actually she had climbed upon the stone until her body completely covered it. There she paused, stretching her tentacles.

Just in front of her lay one of the golden rose petals.

Gradually she extended her head to bring her mouth to this petal and with an audible crunch began to devour it. Meanwhile her three sisters moved to the other petals and munched on them. For a moment I felt I was at the feeding ground of ravenous royal dragons.

This experience approached the bloodcurdling. Henceforth I could never doubt how in all her manifestations the Great Mother feeds upon herself. Nor could I ever doubt her infinite and final power.

*   *   *

This morning there she was again. Amazing: ever reconstituting herself within me, the Worm Queen glides out of me very day. Ah, to make a poem as naturally as a turd!

Struck by the singular potency of this, I knew suddenly what I had to do. I went and fetched my palette plate thick with accumulated paints. Then with my fingers I fished my turd out of the toilet bowl and put it on the plate. This I carried to my table in the sunlight. There quickly I began with both hands to fingerpaint.

It was wildly exhilarating. I made many forms out of my shit. When in time I inadvertently created a Medusa head, I stopped and stared at it and began to laugh.

I went smellily giggling to the shower.

AUGUST 4

In my dream at dawn I stood wearing a sweater, which was not yet finished around the midriff, the needles and the ball of wool still attached to it. Had I to wait till the sweater was entirely knit together before I could set forth?

But then I was told that it was designed to become eventually a coat of many colors. What matter then if you set forth in an incomplete garment with the stitches showing? Maybe it will never be fully knit. So wear what there is, wear what you have. It all comes together in the end, said Annie winding up the wool, and it fills all the spaces in between.

Before breakfast I went to the woods. The Worm Queen was

not there, nor any of her company. There remained not a single vestige of our encounters, nothing except the black stone, which looked today as if it had lain in the forest for decades.

I knelt to pray but the earth felt like the grave of a stranger. And it was cold. I did not linger. I left one rosebud.

*   *   *

Today was the last art class. We made a collage mural together and had doughnuts. Not a breath of wind this afternoon. The sheep in the pasture stand motionless, the Sea lies silent. I find it difficult to get moving.

K. sends another urgent letter: rehearsals for the play begin next Monday. I am trying to pack. I have carefully wrapped up my bloodstone. What will my reality be when I am back in the tumult?

First of all I know I have to get to the dentist, I have to rewrite my last act, and I must find a new place to live. But what about all that has happened here? Where will my Androgyne want to take me now?

*   *   *

At sunset I went down to the Sea to say goodbye. I had picked the most full-blown rose I could find in the garden. In the stillness the Sea scarcely moved and the big tidepool stood crystal clear as I gazed into it.

Old friend, I said, help me to persevere. Keep your depths in me, your heartbeat, and your Yes. Help me to endure the crucifixion of being what I am!

As I spoke I was startled to see a stranger looking up at me.

The Sea laughed ripplingly. Don't you recognize your own secrets, my son? You reflect more than you know. You are your own twin and your own bride and all your gods. As is every man, though he knows it not. Rejoice in oneness while you can. Allness is ripe!

A strange bird came trumpeting around the cliff, skimmed the glassy water, and disappeared. It took my timidity with it.

Clothes and all, I plunged into the tidepool to embrace that other who looked up at me with so much longing. I splashed crazily there till night fell and I could no longer see.

FROM SEEING THE LIGHT

FROM *SEEING THE LIGHT* (1977)

Seeing the Light, Broughton's book on filmmaking, appeared from City Lights in 1977. Rewritten, and with a new title, *Making Light of It*, the book appeared again from City Lights in 1992. The new version began with a glance at Dante's *Vita Nuova*: "On a foggy morning in 1946 Sidney Peterson took me to an abandoned cemetery in San Francisco where I discovered a new life." The selections here are from the 1977 edition. "Follow your own Weird" is Broughton's transmutation of Joseph Campbell's phrase, 'Follow your bliss." As he did with everything, Broughton constantly mythologies cinema, seeing it in relationship not only to himself but to various worlds and contexts:

When I was 30 my greatest consolation was the thought of suicide. But that was three years before I began to make films. What a lot of vicissitude, ecstasy and ennui I would have missed!

Did the creation of moving black and white images save my life? It is certain that I have never seriously contemplated suicide since. "It takes a long time to become young," said Picasso.

* * *

I am not talking here about going to the movies; I am talking about making cinema. I am talking about the life of vision. I am talking about cinema as one way of living the life of a poet. I am talking about film as poetry, as philosophy, as metaphysics, as all else it has not yet dared to become.

* * *

Going to the movies, to indulge your fantasies or to have critical opinions, is certainly one way to pass your time. But it has little to do with the art of bringing the movie to life or bringing life to the movie. Be wary: life is what happens while you are doing something else.

* * *

Analytical theorizing is often felt to be "over one's head." It is nothing of the sort. It is actually under one's feet. It is the mud one has to wade through: the bog of literal minds who build labyrinthine swamps of intellect to preserve themselves from direct experience. What is truly over one's head is the realm of the poetic imagination. As Barnett Newman put it: "Aesthetics is for the artist as ornithology is for the birds."

* * *

Cinema like life is only worth living when it is in the service of something beyond the explicit and the mundane.

When Marianne Moore was asked whether she wrote poetry for fame or for money, she replied, "Are there no other alternatives?"

* * *

Every new film begins from scratch, from a roll of blank film, as if one knew nothing at all. Another leap in the dark, another jump off a cliff!

* * *

Look at cinema as a mystery religion.

Going to the movies is a group ceremony. One enters the darkened place and joins the silent congregation. Like mass, performances begin at set times. You may come and go but you must be quiet, showing proper respect and awe, as in the Meeting House or at Pueblo dances. Up there at the altar space a rite is to be performed, which we are expected to participate in.

* * *

The Secret Name of Cinema is Transformation
        Transform transform
        anything everything—
        stairways into plants
        buttercups into navels

icebergs into elephants—
everything
everywhere
the old scene renewed by seeing
the unseen seen anew
transformed

*   *   *

Are you ready and willing to take the Three Vows—the vows of Poverty, Chastity, and Obedience?

Poverty: because you will be forever in debt to the camera store and the laboratory, and will be forever begging from friends and foundations.

Chastity: because you will be wedded to your work and your wildest escapes will be with it.

Obedience: because your life will be in the service of an endlessly demanding tyrant with more heads that a hydra and more legs than a centipede.

*   *   *

The Pledge

I swear to abstain from all readymade ideas and from all critical assumptions.

I swear to refrain from falling in love with my own footage.

I swear to be precise, ruthless and articulate.

I swear to delight the eye and ear of all creatures.

I swear to attempt the impossible, to exceed myself (no one else), and to venture where no one has ever pushed a button before.

I swear that my aim will always be: to put the right image in the right place at the right time and at the right length.

*   *   *

Don't waste your time making a film like anyone else's. That's duplication of effort. Besides, it won't be any good. Your business is to make something that neither you nor I have ever seen before. Your business is to make a wonderful new kind of mess in your own way... Your business is to take the risk of your madness. Hello, Columbus.

Excellent strategy: do what you are most afraid of doing. Look what [Stan] Brakhage did. He has always feared death intensely; it has been a constant threatening imminence for him. So, with the courage that has always made him a trail-blazer, he took his camera tightly in hand and went into the city morgue of Pittsburgh and looked closely and filmed unforgettably the forms of death as they had never been seen before: The Act of Seeing With One's Own Eyes.

*   *   *

If you become familiar with your dreams, you will enter the translucent realm of the archetypes, those potent primal images of mankind. They are much more exciting and abiding than topical events.

*   *   *

"Follow your own Weird." But this doesn't mean that all you have to do is turn on the camera and express yourself. Just as talking has nothing to do with creating, self-expression has nothing to do with art. "Anything goes" may be therapy but that is only prelude to the shaping of visions thus discovered.

*   *   *

Perhaps the ultimate avant-garde position: to reach the place where you no longer lean on any object, any reference. Or, as with Krishnamurti, 'the stairway without any railing.' Then you might reach the sphere of the innate light, the Mother Light, the light of which all other lights are the children.

Can you go past your dreams to the pure light of dreaming?

*   *   *

For the Brothers of Light Cinema is:
        a high form of yoga discipline

a service of prayer and thanksgiving
a translucent mystery
a devotional agony
a quest for ecstasy
a new creation of the world
a society of explorers
a fellowship of the inner radiance

* * *

In recent years some particularly movie characters have moved into Oz. One of them is a dowager from the early days, Queen Trixie of Flix, who dwells in the Hall of the Great Silents. She has gotten fat from long sitting, her eyesight is defective, and she no longer knows one movie from another. But her magic movieola is always going and she loves everything she sees.

One of the muses of cinema sometimes visits Queen Trixie of Flix: a shadowy alluring creature, who has a habit of fading out when you need her most, her name is Oblivia. She makes filmmakers obvious of everything but film and then leads them and their works into oblivion.

Some of the other muses of cinema are: Lumena, Opia, Ephemera, Insomnia, Nostalgia, and Synchronicita.

Above all of these is, of course, the great goddess CineMa, whom the residents of Cineoz worship religiously. She is a goddess of Time continually weaving for us and through us the fabric of her illusions of the world. All the movies that we imagine we experience in time are generated for us by her dancing web. Endlessly proliferating, she is our mother, our magic and our despair.

* * *

Some Mottos for Editing Room Walls (1992 version)
Compose yourself. Then compose.
Every frame is a moment of Now.
Take nothing for granted.

By all means try all means.
When in doubt, cut.
Attain the inevitable.
Allness is ripe.

*   *   *

Cinema is its own *Book of Changes*. It has, in the end, little to do with works of art as such. It is not an infinite number of separate "things." It is a "sensitive chaos" in duration like the Tao [In Chinese philosophy, the absolute principle underlying the universe, combining within itself the principles of yin and yang, and signifying the way or code of behavior, that is in harmony with the natural order—ed.]. How can you look at something as a public monument when, while you are looking at it, it is already floating down the river into Elsewhere? … the picture you just took of what is happening is not what is happening now.

*   *   *

The Tao of cinema affirms unbroken movement: it never stops, it never turns back, its patterns are real only as they pass. And every observer is himself part of this weblike river. This is the never-ceasing cinema of our light and dark, great and small, dim and bright Yang and Yin.

*   *   *

If you accept the principal of Eternal Change as governing the universe, then to work in a perishable medium like film means that you accept the universe…. Either you trust a river, or you don't. Tao means knowing that you don't know, and being happy about it.

*   *   *

There is no black and white dualism in Taoist cinema. Its dark is always into its light and its light is always into its dark, for these are not absolutes. They continually flow into one another, overlap, become their opposites. This is symbolized on the revolving reel of the *Tai Chi* [Chinese martial art and system of calisthenics, consisting of sequences of very slow controlled movements—ed], at the beginning and ending of *Nuptiae*. That symbol is the eternal movie of the Relative Absolute (or Absolute Relative), which might best be expressed by a transcendental double exposure.

Is there a true Taoist film that uses double exposure metaphysically to reveal the play of opposites in every moment of our being? Please try this, someone.

*   *   *

Buddhistically speaking, cinema is just a way of filling the Void.

*   *   *

From the *Potted Psalm* in 1946 to *Erogeny* in 1976 I could not have created anything without sharing love with my collaborators. This is a weakness I take delight in. "Relations are real, not substances," said the Buddha. And the more intense the love, the livelier the work. Eros is a true source of the Light.

*   *   *

All of my own films have been acts of love. They have been made with love and for love, with the love of others and for those whom I loved. And for the most part the theme of all my work is Love: a call for, a quest for, a fete for.

I meant what I said in Testament: I do believe in ecstasy for everyone. There is nothing I would more gladly give to the world, if I could. The ecstatic has been my faith and my adventure.

THROWING SOME LIGHT ON THE SUBJECT

James Broughton on his Films

THROWING SOME LIGHT ON THE SUBJECT
JAMES BROUGHTON ON HIS FILMS

I am here to acquire a little more multi for my media.

*   *   *

Film is very hot stuff.

— James Broughton,
Film Culture (No. 61, 1975-76)

The following remarks were originally published in Film Culture's James Broughton issue (No. 61, 1975-76), though I have amplified them with selections from Broughton's book, *Making Light of It* (1992) and other sources. These selections are in brackets. Broughton's descriptions sometimes differ slightly from the completed film. This is particularly true in the case of *Dreamwood*. Nevertheless, the remarks give a good sense of his intentions and of the kinds of thoughts that occurred to him as he was actually conceiving a film. I have taken the title of this section from one of James's high kukus. Broughton's attempts to use "poems as shooting scripts" in *Four in the Afternoon* represents one of many attempts to bring together various separate aspects of his personality. Film itself is the intersection point of various media.

MOTHER'S DAY (1948)
(A family album in six parts)

Mother's Day (1948) 23 min. B/W 16mm sound
Written and directed by James Broughton.
Assistant director: Kermit Sheets.
Photography: Frank Stauffacher.
Music by Howard Brubeck.

[In *Coming Unbuttoned* Broughton writes, "Adults engaged in childish behavior had been the device I used for the political allegory of The Playground. At first I had considered using that play as a scenario but as soon as we began filming in the alleys and backyards of the city nostalgic memories seemed to walk right onto the set and evoke the bewilderments of my own growing up. "Soon I had to ask: how could I re-create the truth of my San Francisco childhood without the Severe Eminence of my mother at the center of it? To portray the mother I chose one of my most beautiful friends, a talented pastelist from Bakersfield, because she possessed the iconic placidity of a silent movie star, Marion Osborn Cunningham did not attempt to act, she was simply there. Her presence dominated the film, which is how it acquired the ironic title of *Mother's Day*." In *Seeing the Light* he adds, "The adults in *Mother's Day* are looking for a lost Oz."]

A capricious but unsparing souvenir of a San Francisco childhood, recalled in the nostalgic style of a cluttered family album, this film exposes the fetishes and enigmas and secret nonsense rituals of a large household dominated by a self-absorbed mother with a taste for exotic hats and stereotyped children.

Although it is a film of unhappy memories revisited, wherein adults absurdly reenact their infancy by playing as they did while growing up, the focus is upon the tyranny of the mother's misguided romanticism. She who thinks of herself as a frail Victorian miniature, but is actually voluptuous and severe in the flesh, finds no real human being acceptable to her, so that when the children have mocked her and rebelled, she is left alone in riding boots with nowhere to ride to.

But she would explain her history thus: "Once upon a time there was a very beautiful and refined young girl who had a great many suitors. But she married the wrong one. Then she had a great many children and she did not know what to do with them either."

The Argument

Every child's mother who was once a child is usually obliged to grow up and to alter her toys. But often there are certain cherished old playthings—a window, a mirror, a scrapbook—which she wishes could refuse to alter. And she may also regret in each new picture-game of her children how the play of their reflections alters her. (Images like these tend to provoke a rather askew nostalgia.)

However much she may desire her mirror to tell her she is still a princess, she can see for herself how fairy tales go awry. She may even grow into a kind of witch-queen, when she can no longer play the fairy godmother with her children's own fancies. To say nothing of their father becoming a real ogre, who likes to order all the windows shut.

And if she wants her children to keep her scrapbook, and to illustrate it, they seldom picture it the way she sees it. Or they merely find it diverting. For as they grow up to the mirror, they open their own windows. And when they overtake her toys and begin to collect her into their own souvenirs, she may be left unwillingly to repicture her scrapbook.

For her favorite bedtime story is apt to remain: "Once upon a time there was a very beautiful and refined young girl who had a great many suitors. But she married the wrong one. Then she had a great many children and she did not know what to do with them either."

Part I

Subtitle: *Mother was the loveliest woman in the world. And Mother wanted everything to be lovely.*

This is a formal prelude, announcing the central theme of the entire film. The mother sees herself as a delicate old miniature. But when we come close to her we encounter the voluptuous severity of her actual presence. And we see her confront the images of her obsessive romanticism, and watch her turn away toward the inevitable despair of their defeat.

Part II

Subtitle: *Mother always said that she could have had her pick.*

This is Mother's story of herself to herself: the princess in the tower sought after by all the princes of the town, none of whom was good enough for her. And this is acted out as if by children parodying an adult legend, with the toys and the tricks they have at hand; as if this is the way Mother's story of her girlhood sounds to her mischievous son.

Part III

Subtitle: *And she picked Father.*

The tragic mistake: explosion of the miniature, the mirror invaded by the stern parent-husband, and with it comes motherhood that can only be accepted as a little girl's passion for dressing dolls.

Part IV

Subtitle: *Then Mother always said she wanted little boys and girls to be lovely.*

The playlife of the children (who are the same age as the mother) is a constant source of Mother's envy and disapproval, since their sportive discovery recalls her own lost playmates and unfound joys.

Part V

Subtitle: *Because ladies and gentlemen were the loveliest thing in the world.*

Going to parties, or inventing parties of their own, the children make fun of grownup behavior or find their own fun misbehaving behind the backs of the grownups.

Part VI

Subtitle: *And so we learned how to be lovely too.*

The children take over Mother's own objects and transform her way of life into something for their own lives. While Father is turned upside down on the wall, she is left behind in an empty room, still dressed to go out but with nowhere to go.

The Style

Everything herein that moves and turns is an act of play. For everything herein is concerned with the forays, the fears, and the aftermaths of play, even the most unfrivolous matters.

Children play-act at being adults. Adults play at being adults and act like children.

Child play can be deadly serious, devilish mockery, or light-hearted improvisation. Adults (like Mother) play just as hard but more obsessively and with less happy results all around.

A toy is a real thing, but it is also whatever property the imagination may want to make it. And the world is full of objects revolving before the wondering eyes of the newcomers: all the toys that are the paraphernalia of our lives.

Herein the play and the toys deal with something that cannot finally be understood: the enigmas of emotional relationships and the mysterious perversity of human behavior. The only clue to resolving these, since we cannot understand one another, is love and acceptance.

*   *   *

TWO NOTES ON *MOTHER'S DAY*

Note One:

From the beginning I accepted the camera's sharply accurate eye as a value rather than a limitation. The camera's challenge to the poet is that his images must be as definite as possible: the magic of his persons, landscapes, and actions occurring in an apparent reality. At this point something approaching choreography must enter in: the finding of meaningful gesture and movement. And from the beginning I decided to make things happen head on, happen within frame, without vagueness, without camera trickery—so that it would be how the scenes were made to happen in front of the lens, and then how they were organized in the montage, that would evoke the world I wanted to explore.

The subject matter of *Mother's Day* cannot, certainly, be considered specialized. Most of us have had some experience of childhood.... But do we remember that children are often incomprehensibly terror-stricken, are always ready to slip over into some private nonsense-ritual, or into behavior based upon their misconception of the adult world? Furthermore, what about the "childish behavior" of grown-ups, their refusal to relinquish childhood misconceptions, or to confront the world they inhabit?

Although this film is, then, by its very nature, a nostalgic comedy, it eschews chronological accuracy in either the period details or the dramatic events. It has been one of the clichés of cinema since the days of cubism that the medium allows the artist to manipulate time: to cut it up, retard or accelerate it, and so forth. In *Mother's Day*, historical time may be said to stand still. Periods and fashions are gently scrambled. The device is deliberate: for with this film we are in the country of emotional memory, where everything may happen simultaneously.

This is because the basic point of vision of the film is that of an adult remembering the past (and the past within the past): projecting himself back as he is now, and seeing his family and his playmates at his present age-level, regarding them with adult feelings and knowledge, and even projecting them forward into his present-day concerns.

But also there is, as it were, a double exposure of memory in the film though its springboard is the remembering of childhood, it more deeply involves the mother's remembering of her own life: her desires and regrets toward her own playmates, her disappointments in marriage, her envy that her children take over her romantic illusions on their own terms and inevitably leave her behind.

Since this is a film about families, about privacy and society, it repeatedly uses the image of the circle and, as Parker Tyler has pointed out, the object revolving on a fixed axis. The use of headgear (about which I am so often questioned) is merely an extension of these visual metaphors.

The choice of actors all of relatively the same age to act the parts of both children and grown-ups was a means of maintaining throughout the film that uncertain borderland of conflict between being a child and being a grown-up, as well as to implicate the world of the mother in the world of infantile daydream—she being, in the case of this particular family album, perhaps the biggest child of them all. The only exceptions to this casting—the figures of two older women—are projections of her fear of time and of possible event.

Note Two:

The subject matter in *Mother's Day* is both cultural and personal. I make these distinctions because the themes of two of my books meet and cross in this film. In my verse play, *The Playground*, I have pictured adults acting like children within a frame of reference to our social and psychological "childish behavior": the refusal to confront the world we live in. And in *Musical Chairs* I have presented in a series of poems a record of the inner state. The subtitle of that volume is "A Songbook for Anxious Children."

In *Mother's Day* I deliberately used adults acting as children, to evoke the sense of projecting oneself as an adult back into memory, to suggest the impossible borderline between when one is child and when one is grown-up, and to implicate Mother in the world of the child fantasies as being, perhaps, the biggest child of them all—since she, in this case, has never freed herself from narcissistic daydreams...

The hats are another (and more graphic) means of referring to finding what shoe to fit for following in parental footsteps, as they also serve nicely as traditional symbols for changes in fashion and social changes.

The visual style of *Mother's Day* is based on play. The film is concerned with aspects and aftermaths of play. The spirit of play is the key to the order of images, for the actions—even when they are dealing with the most unfrivolous matters—are conceived in terms of play.

The objects that persons find in their world, explore, reject, or use in their rituals, are to be thought of as toys: the paraphernalia of play. Like all playthings they are as actual as they are symbolic. They are toys in the game everyone plays or tries—the long, busy game of growing up.

The play of a child can be profoundly serious, or a devilish mockery, or a light-hearted improvisation. And adults (like Mother) play just as hard, but more obsessively and with less happy results all around.

A toy is a real thing, but it is also whatever property for the imagination one may want to make it. And the world is full of objects of wonder revolving about the questing and puzzled eyes of the newcomer to it, suggestive of many mysteries and destinies, and for him to use or make what he can of them: the toys of our lives. We have toys at all our seven ages, though we may not acknowledge them so.

ADVENTURES OF JIMMY (1950)

[In *Coming Unbuttoned* Broughton writes, "Another film grew out of the only poem of mine ever accepted by the New Yorker: 'A Lad from the Cold Country'."

When I dwelt in the wood in a wind-cracked hut,
(at a waterwheel pinch the rivers flow)
I seldom bothered the shutters to shut,
for the northern maids are the warmingest, O.

But when I came on to the company town
(at a waterwheel pinch the river flow)
I hastened to pull the shades all down,
for the midlands maids are the harmingest, O.

But when I moved down to the shore of the sea
(at a waterwheel pinch the rivers flow)
I threw the doors open fancy and free,
for the southern maids are the charmingest, O.

… Here I spoofed the classic adolescent adventure as well as making a joke of my own misguided efforts to grow up straight… I called the film *Adventures of Jimmy* since Jimmy was the nickname I had discarded in my twenties. When I fled from Stanford (University) I thereafter called myself James (as in Saint and King) hoping that would give my persona more maturity…. (Later,) in July of 1954 I discovered an affinity for my namesake saint, James the son of Zebedee, patron of Spain, alchemists, and explorers. I adopted his scallop shell and his pilgrim staff as my own emblems."]

Adventures of Jimmy (1950)
11 min. B/W 16mm sound
Written and directed by James Broughton.
Photography: Frank Stauffacher.
Editing: Kermit Sheets.
Music: Weldon Kees.
Sound: Hy Hirsh.
Title role enacted by James Broughton.

An amorous fable in pseudo-documentary style, this is an off-hand parody of the maladjusted Hero, here typified by the unhappy innocent in the Big City searching for his ideal mate. Jimmy, child of the backwoods, discovers the confusions and pressures of a metropolis: he is stalked by ladies of the town, he lodges in the slums, exhausts himself in a dance hall, tries prayer and poetry and psychoanalysis. Thanks to his naïve persistence, his quest proves alarmingly successful: he returns to his cabin with a nice harem.

* * *

CLOUDS : Nothing in life is more important than finding
    what one wants. But this often requires a little effort. To
    begin with, I was just like anybody else.
    Except that I was more of an idealist.

HOUSE : My family died when I was young, and left me
    their entire estate. They left me alone there too.

CLOSEUP: And I had to make out as best I could myself.

CHOPS WOOD: I was a perfectly normal boy. Except that
    I had no one to play with. Besides, I was very awkward
    at doing things. So I wasn't good at games. Of course,
    I hadn't had much practice at them. Having only my
    dreams to work with.

TREES: It's not very romantic when there's only yourself to
    play with. It can also drive you crazy.

PHOTOS: What I wanted more than anything in the world
was a playmate of my own.

SNAPSHOTS:

RISING: I had worried about this problem long enough.
Anyone could see I was nearly
Full grown. It was also obvious I would never get
anywhere staying around here.
So one day I made up my mind to set out in the world
and see what I could find, before it was too late.
I left my home behind and started on my journey—
making my way as best I could.

CANOE:

RIVER: And how easy it was to start a new life! The world
did not seem unfriendly at first. Except that I had to go
a long way before I saw anyone.

AFTER LOOKING THROUGH TELESCOPE: At first glance,
the seashore seemed rather promising. I decided to stay
a while and try my luck. But—which one?
How to choose? Of course, anyone might suffice. But
which was the right one?
Could I make this fit the picture I had in mind?
Black Screen: But one mustn't be easily daunted.

TRAIN: I traveled on to the company town. The city is a
legendary place of opportunity. For those with courage.
Cities are also full of ugliness and lonesome streets. But
one can find beauty anywhere. And I was determined to
look for beauty everywhere.

WHORES: Then, Black Screen.

HORSE: Was there no place for an awkward fellow with
high ideals?

BOARDING HOUSE SIGN:

COMING DOWN STAIRS: Beauty may be found ready-made. But one must also help to make it.

AFTER CINDERELLA: Black: Was I too refined? Too well-read? Or just unattractive?

BICYCLE: Was I, perhaps, going about this the wrong way?

BOYS: So that I gave the wrong impression.

BILLBOARD: But I had to keep trying. Even if I had to try everything.

"PRAYER":

BACK OF HEAD: It was hard for me to be jolly. I still had a long way to go. And I was always at a crossroads. I got anxious. Was loveliness all an illusion?

DANCE:

AFTER TURKISH BATHS: Then, Black Screen. I was getting more confused.

AUTO: Everything led down a blind alley. Was there no one to turn to? And I wasn't feeling very well either.

DR. S—:

BUILDINGS: I felt I was coming to the end of my rope. My future looked dark.

GLASSES: Was there no light that would restore my faith? Didn't I have any destiny?
There was just one thing left to try.

ANALYST:

TREES: With harem. So you see—although it does require a little effort—eventually one can find what one really wants in life.

FOUR IN THE AFTERNOON (1951)

[In *Coming Unbuttoned* Broughton writes, "I had believed Mother's Day would be the only film I would ever make, but when I took the Battered Bolex [camera] into my own hands I wanted to explore a more fluid form of cinema, using poems as shooting scripts. As far as I knew no one had ever done this before.

"I wanted to see a cinema that would dance to words. I wanted to unite my two passions, poetry and dance, into something magical. I had always wanted to dance impossible dances. As a boy I would turn on the Victrola, shed my clothes, and dance dance dance. Till my mother came storming in...

"*Four in the Afternoon* gratified another of my passions [as well]: statuary both sculpted and posed...

"The Gardener's Son hoses down replicas of classical goddesses in Sutro Gardens, still in those days an unmanicured remnant of a once private estate overlooking the Pacific. My Aunt Esto had first taken me there when I was a boy. That initial encounter with sculptures of the gods haunted my life for years and deeply affected all my work in cinema. No wonder I loved Renaissance Italy when I finally encountered it.

"The pseudo-classical Palace of Fine Arts where Princess Printemps is pursued around massive pillars had been another of my childhood dream places. At the time of our filming the plaster of Paris was falling from the dome and the grounds were boarded up. I had to get entry permission from the Parks Department, who allowed me only one day's access."]

Four in the Afternoon (1951)
15 min. B/W 16mm sound
Written, directed and photographed by James Broughton
Assistant director: Kermit Sheets.
Music by William O. Smith.
Voices: Madeline Gleason, James Broughton
Performers: dancers Anna Halprin and Welland Lathrop with members of their company and actors.

This is a film suite in four parts based upon poems in the book, *Musical Chairs* (1950). Each movement of this quartet is a variation on the theme of the quest for love, embodying forms of desire at crucial age levels from the child of 10 to the man of 40, and extending in mood from the farcical to the elegiac. Like a lyric poem each section compresses the essence of a realm of feeling into a compact moment, blending image, music, dance, and spoken verse. The movements are:

1) Game Little Gladys, in which her magic skipping game conjures all the possible knights a little girl of 10 might choose for her partner.

2) The Gardener's Son, in which a lad of 20 indulges his rapturously imprecise daydreams of clothed and unclothed goddesses.

3) Princess Printemps, in which a moonstruck female of 30 is pursued by an eager male on a flirtatious romp around a huge classic ruin.

4) The Aging Balletomane, in which a middle-aged man of 40 in a squalid backyard evokes visions of lost romance and youthful sprightliness.

Each movement is itself a poetic movement.

Each movement blends its movement with music and verse.

First Movement (Allegro): *Game Little Gladys*

Gladys, 10, escaping out the back door with her jump rope, comes skipping down the stairs, down all the stairs in the town, down to what is her reality: the guessing game her heart plays over the wall, down upon the foundations of an old building.

There about eagerly she skips her rope, conjuring all her possible knights, who magically appear upon the pediments as she counts:

One two three,
my bonnet has a bee.

Four five six,
my bag is full of tricks.

Seven eight nine,
my twinkletoe is shines.

Ten is the number
of the husbands in my heart.

Which one will count me
His true sweetheart?

All ten are of all possible romantic shapes. Swinging her rope, she goes closer to observe her heroes. But each one disappears as she approaches him.

Oh well! She'll be back tomorrow. It's a game that she's sure to win someday. Irrepressible skipper, off she goes to other games.

Second Movement (Adagio): *The Gardener's Son*

He dreams more than he labors, this gardening boy of 20. For he is beset by all the yearning squirms of youthful spring. And he has delicious visions among the bushes and the statuary. Everywhere he looks he sees lovely ladies—undressed nymphs, well dressed strollers, a girl in a tree, a girl on a toadstool, an Alice walking away into her own wonderland. As he clears the vines and hoses Diana, it is never clear whether all women are statues or all statues are women.

But, as he goes on his rounds around the Venus de Milo, we can hear how his heart thumps and his desires speak:

I have cap, I have trouser,
I have tears yet to learn
on mountain and meadow
where foxes still woo.
I have shovel and planting
for a loam way to travel,
till I bed a wild dove
when the rose is new.

Pure will blow my love,
honeyed will she be:
O what beautifying of the bee   !

Then I shall snip the link
of the snail-sender's shrink
and the statue with clean sleeves,
I shall skip the foxes too.
So mock not my greensleeves,
for I will queen a kingdom
I will mate a ringdove
when the rose is new.
> Pure will blow my love,
> honeyed will she be:
> O what beautifying of the bee!

Third Movement (Scherzo): *Princess Printemps*

In the doorway of a ruined palace a skittish female of 30, dressed like a foolish fugitive from Watteau turns fluttering toward us, and thinking herself unobserved, pantomimes what she has to say:

Spring
> spring
>> runs round a green riddle,
follows a round robin cruel and gay.
> The virgins of April heed
> the call of the leapfrog
and go on a roundtrip till the middle of May—
> for the sons of Apollo
> rush out to shoot apples
around the round riddle
>> hey diddle
>> hooray!

She parodies a courtly dance, and twitchily carried away by it leaps into the air and runs about the gardens of the huge ruin, waving to the swans and peeking through the columns. She is gone quite daft with undifferentiated longing.

Like a slightly demented and aging sprite, she lopes among the roses, tries one in her teeth, and goes sighing off sideways—right past a limber courtier, lounging against a pediment in the moonlight. He, smitten on the immediate, promptly makes the overture:

He

How do you do, miss maiden,
and how do I dance with you?
In view of the criss-cross eye of the moon,
do you mind if I ask, Who are you?

She
(all over girlish)
I would if I could, but I can't.
I'm not always myself, you know.

He

But many a duo can double as one
if it crosses its I with its me.
From my point of view of the kiss-eyed moon,
which one is you and who's thee?

She
I could if I would, but I won't.
I'm not always myself, you know.

He

But all the world's ones come out by twos
for a four-legged waltz of whom and who.
By the double-cross moon, do you mind if I ask,
who who, miss maiden, are you?

She
(with an over the shoulder wink)
I should if I did, but I shan't.
I'm not always myself, you know.

And off she runs delighted to be the fox, making sure the hunter is in pursuit. He chases her up and over and under the urns and arches.

He chases She—until growing tireder and tireder, they move slower and slower. Yet far on into the night and forever, he pursues her around the Corinthian pillar. Dogtired, hair down, and shoeless, she still sings it:

Spring
          spring
                    runs round a green riddle,
follows a round robin cruel and gay.
          The virgins of April heed
          the call of the leapfrog
and go on a roundtrip till the middle of May—
          for the sons of Apollo
          rush out to shoot apples
around the round riddle
                              hey diddle
                              hooray!

Fourth Movement (Lento): *The Aging Balletomane*

[This takes place, writes Broughton, "in the untidy backyard of 1724 Baker Street."] Chair-rocking alone in his squalid backyard, among the old sheets hanging out on the line, the middle-aged dancer of 40 clings to his memories of the past, the days of youth, the visions of romance:

Once I had wild geese to keep me flying—
no creaking toes nor needled eyes
like these in the now rain sighing.
          O ago so long, alas!

Fleetly in bird shoes I led and I leapt
(my raven girl whirling a red-cloud skirt)
and there were no mists where I wept.
          O in the days when we danced!

He manages to conjure up the ballerina of his dreams, right there in the tenement backyard. She floats up onto an old stool and begins her Swan Lake variation. But it is all done backward. As all the movement in this movement is aimed backward. The

balletomane himself runs more rapidly backward as
if this is the only way he can move forward.

At the height of his desire for the apparition,
she vanishes. And then he tries, with his opera glasses
and with an old mirror, to bring her back, to bring
something like her back:
Shall my feet now rust in a barnyard rain?
or might by chance one last high goose
come flying this chase again?
          O ago so long, how it passed!

He settles back into his curlicue rocker, the lost dream still gleaming
in his eye.

LOONY TOM, THE HAPPY LOVER (1951)
(an homage to Mack Sennett)

Loony Tom, The Happy Lover (1951)
11 min. B/W 16mm sound
Written, directed, and photographed by James Broughton.
Music by Ralph Gilbert.
Title role enacted by Kermit Sheets.

This comedy pictures the amorous progress of a prancing, baggy-
trousered, bowler-hatted, demented and blissfully happy tramp, who
capers across a sunlit countryside making immediate and outrageous
love to every woman he encounters. He disrupts an artist's idyll,
cuddles a country wife, chases a bevy of milkmaids, lays a stern widow
on the floor, and blithely goes singing on his way.

The style is derived from silent slapstick comedies, with pantomimic
rhythms, hectic situations, and exaggerated postures. But the theme
celebrates something lyrical and vital: it is an impudent testimony to

the liberating spirit of Pan and the pleasures of being alive.

* * *

If you were a baggy-panted Pan, with a battered bowler and an unquenchable gleam in the eye, who slept in the bushes and spent every waking hour daftly pursuing any female who passed, what would you sing as you pranced? Would it be anything like Tom?

> Give me a tune and I'll slap the bull fife,
> I'll spring the hornblower out of his wife.
>
> Any old flutist you care to uncover,
> Give me his name and I'll be her lover.
>
>> La diddle la, the hydrant chatted.
>> Um titty um, the milkpail said.
>
> For love hid the story under the songbook,
> Buried the ballad under the horn book.
>
> Love so they tell me, love so I hear,
> Love waves the trumpet and butters the tree.
>
> But love will come tooting only if free.
> And only to me.
>
>> La diddle la, the hydrant chatted.
>> Um titty um, the milkpail said.

THE PLEASURE GARDEN (1953)

The Pleasure Garden (1953)
38 min. B/W 16mm sound
(Originally filmed in 35mm)
Written and directed by James Broughton.
Assistant director: Kermit Sheets.
Photography: Walter Lassally.
Music by Stanley Bate.
Production Manager: Lindsay Anderson.
Produced by Flights of Fancy Committee for Farallone Films.
Featured actors: Hattie Jacques, John Le Mesurier, Diana Maddox, Jean Anderson.

Produced in England under the aegis of the British Film Institute, this is a comic fantasy with songs that celebrates the triumph of love and liberty over the joyless forces of restriction.

A large romantically dilapidated park lies under the yoke of a puritanical Minister of Public Behavior who is determined that none of the visitors shall enjoy themselves. The pleasure-seekers who come there are an odd lot, all lovelorn and given to acting out their daydreams: a girl who wants to be a beautiful statue, a sculptor trying to find reality in abstractions, a bird-watching widow, a pretty cyclist hoping to run down a husband, a maiden singing of her sailor at the bottom of the sea, a roving cowboy, a long distance walker with no destination, a lonely girl named Bess chaperoned by a formidable aunt.

Having made them all unhappier than they already were, the funereal Minister then tries to expel the idlers and turn the garden into a cemetery. However, a portly and waggish fairy godmother named Dr. Mary Albion comes to their rescue with some impish magical tricks and thereby launches a full rebellion against all killjoys and unites the lost lovers.

["Filmed in the ruins of the Crystal Palace Gardens," Broughton adds in *Making Light of It*, "this celebration of love included a large company of professional actors and a 35mm cameraman, Walter Lassally. To my astonishment it gained a special prize at the Cannes Festival in 1954."]

THE BED (1968)

["Recently (in 1967, the San Francisco "Summer of Love")," Broughton writes in *Coming Unbuttoned*, "I have become obsessed by beds, by the bed as humanity's most enjoyable article of furniture. I had written 'a play in four bedrooms' called Bedlam: four undressed dramas occurring concurrently in four Modesto locations. I had even proposed a revue called *Beds* to Herbert Blau at his Actors' Workshop. Neither of these projects had reached production stage. Therefore in considering a film... I devised scenes for a romp of the human comedy enacted on a bed in an open-air Eden ... when it was finally edited I could not persuade any commercial laboratory to print it. From Eastman in Rochester to Consolidated in Los Angeles I received curt refusals: it was against official policy to print 'frontal nudity.' Finally I located an illegal pornography outfit, which printed much frontal nudity between midnight and dawn in the rear of a building on a back street in East Palo Alto.

"To my astonishment *The Bed* won many prizes at world festivals. Furthermore it broke a taboo: frontal nudity soon populated all avant-garde screens. Only two years later my subsequent project, totally nude *Golden Positions*, encountered no difficulty with any printer. To my further astonishment, *The Bed* came into widespread use as a relaxing introduction to consciousness-raising seminars and training programs for social, hospital, and psychiatric workers." In *Seeing the Light* (1977) Broughton adds:

> When I made *The Bed* I thought it ... was a one and only last picture show. I had not made a film for 13 years and I was prodded into 'just one more' by Jacques Ledoux of the Belgian Film Archive for his international experimental powwow of 1968. All I did was express how life felt to me in my 50's. *The Bed* has no special style, there isn't a trick in it, it is all straight cuts. I wanted to show as directly as possible my vision of the flowing river of existence and I thought of it as a private communication to an old friend in Brussels. The public success of the film astounded me.]

The Bed (1968)
20 min. Color 16mm sound
Written, directed by James Broughton
Camera: Bill Desloge. Music: Warner Jepson.
With Alan Watts, Gavin Chester, Imogen Cunningham, Grover Sales, Jean Varda, Herb Beckman, Wes Wilson, Betty Fuller, John Graham, Roger Somer.

* * *

Argument: All the world's a bed, and men and women merely dreamers.

<h3 align="center">A Synopsis</h3>

Prologue

Descending into a valley, like some Occidental vehicle of the Tao, flows a spry but monumental Bed—as if to proclaim, "In the beginning God created the bed, and sent it down to earth."

When the bed comes to rest in a primeval woodland, an echo of Creation is evoked upon it with the innocent playfulness of Eden.

This is followed by an invocation of certain eternal guardians of man's dream: the satyr, the seer, the serpent, the magic circle, and the angel.

Part I: *Inner Reality*

The bed is dressed by a vestal attendant. Then upon it the mystery of life is laid by an aged earth mother.

Clothed young people frozen in wonder and uncertainty contemplate the bed. Upon it they envision their collective dreams, taboos, and transformations. Ultimately the instinctual call of Pan releases them into action.

Part II: *Outer Reality*

The games that older humans play upon the bed of their lives is suggested by a sequence of couples in varied rituals. This culminates in the eternal return to the mother and the last rites of death, followed

by an image of the greatest of all mysteries: the hermaphroditic union
of the opposites.

Epilogue

In a coda, the bed is remade for the everlasting line of humanity
still to come, play their parts, and move on.

The film closes with a restatement of its theme of unity in life, and
the bed rolls on to another incarnation.

SONG OF THE BED

O everything important in life
      occurs upon a bed.
It's where you cry when you are born
      and where you lie when dead.

You spend a third of your life in bed
      with sickness, sex and sleeping.
You can have a good laugh with your love in bed
      though it's also used for weeping.

In a bed the most fantastic things
      are hoped for and conceived.
It's where you dream, it's where you scheme,
      and where you are deceived.

It's where on earth you come to birth
      and most of childhood spend.
It's where you come and where you don't
      and where you come to an end.

NUPTIAE (1969)

[In *Making Light of It*, Broughton writes, "Since he was present
as best man, [filmmaker] Stan Brakhage had insisted that I let him film
the three ceremonies of my wedding to Suzanna Hart in 1961: at the

City Hall, at the altar and privately at the seashore. This footage formed the basis for what I later developed into Nuptiae." Broughton adds in *Coming Unbuttoned*, "For two theater-trained graduates of Jungian mythologies the only way either of us could accept the marriage was to think of it as a major performance piece embellished with enough flair to impress ourselves that it was for real."

> All marriages require arrangement of some kind. And even a sissy can walk to an altar. The Jungians had convinced me where my mother had failed. Their argument used fancier terms: one could not achieve psychic wholeness until one had outgrown being a puer and undergone the initiation of an alchemical coniunctio. In other words, only by belittling the energies of Pan and Peter Pan and agreeing to cohabit and copulate could one attain the desirable conformity my mother had cherished. In my case, aside from being a surrender to the maw of the Great Mother, could wedlock justify the cost of my analysis, surprise my friends, and gratify (Stan) Brakhage? He had said that he would like to see me as happy with Suzanna as he was with [his wife] Jane. Though weary of the anxieties of singleness I wondered whether I was sufficiently individuated to take on the anxieties of coupling.

Later, James and Suzanna "discovered new roles to play: Papa and Mama. A daughter we named Serena was born on the day of JFK's assassination. Two years later she was joined by a brother we named Orion…. Parenthood turned me into a more serious wage earner. In the Creative Arts Department at San Francisco State University I taught cinema studies and ritual magic."]

Nuptia (1969)
14 1/2 min. Color 16mm sound
Written and directed by James Broughton.
Photography: Stan Brakhage.
Music: Lou Harrison.
Priest: Alan Watts.

This is a celebration of wedding and being wed, poetically amplifying three actual ceremonies: secular, spiritual, and individual ways of initiation into the uniting of opposites. It is a film of ritual magic, with Yang and the Yin forever turning and the Alchemical Mystery forever transforming.

THE GOLDEN POSITIONS (1970)

[In *Making Light of It* Broughton writes, "Naked human bodies in movement have always entranced me. In attempting a pseudo-documentary of undressed humanity I took inspiration from the pioneer studies of Edweard Muybridge, from Alan Watts telling me that Confucius considered standing, sitting, and lying the golden positions of life, and from the Catholic Mass as the form to parody for this celebration of the holiness of the physical body, I filmed a variety of naked persons in various tableaus of the three positions, including the creation of Adam, a swift history of art, religion and social behavior, with a finale of sublime erotic poses. For this last section a chorus sings a kyrie."]

The Golden Positions (1970)
32 min. Color 16mm sound
Written, directed, edited and narrated by James Broughton.
Assistant director: Kermit Sheets.
Photography: Fred Padula.
Music: Composed by Robert Hughes. Performed by the Berkeley Chamber Singers, with Miriam Abramowitch, soprano; conducted by Alden Gilchrist.
With Anna Halprin, James Brunot, Norma Leistiko, and other members of the Dancers' Workshop.

* * *

I—The Lesson
(Voice of the Preacher):

Let us contemplate.
The lesson for today is "The Body of Man,"
that remarkably constructed mystery
which is the measure of all things
and the proper study of mankind.

To know the body more intimately
let us examine its customary positions.

Ancient philosophy tells us that in the normal life of man
the body requires three positions.

Let us illustrate.

This position is standing.
Observe the body standing.
How nobly it stands on feet.
Standing is man's crowning position.
Man is the highest type of animal in existence.

This is the body sitting.
How neatly it sits on seat.
Most animals find sitting uncomfortable.
Man, however, can sit indefinitely.
Certain cultures consider sitting the most profound position.

Here we have the body lying.
Lying is the body's fundamental position.
How lovely it lieth down.
Lying comes naturally to all animals
Man may be said to have made an art of lying.

Standing, sitting and lying are known in Buddhism
as the Three Dignities of Man.
Thoughtful Confucius called them The Golden Positions.

II—Anthem, in madrigal form
(during credits)
(Chorus):

> Standing standing
> it standeth standing
> How nobly it stands on feet!

> Sitting sitting
> it sitteth sitting
> How neatly it sits on seat!

> Lying lying
> it lieth lying.
> How lovely it lieth down!
> How lovely lying down!

III—Creation of the Body
(Voice of the Preacher):

> Glory be to the Body of Everybody.
> As it was to begin with
> let us pray it will continue.
> O Man!

(During creation and movements of First Man and First Woman):
(Chorus):

> Ave Body!
> Our body … (repeated)
> Ave Ave
> Body Body
> and all the parts thereof.

IV—A Swift History of Art and Religion
(Adam and Eve to Pieta)
(Chorus) burbling:
(At end, they sing:)

Ave Ave
Body Body
and the three positions of.

V—Secular Life

(Voice):

> For being able to live up to our daily positions,
> dear Body, we thank thee and raise thee.

(Chorus) litany:

> For being able to arise in the morning,
> dear Body, we thank thee
> and wash thee.

> For being able to stand up to our daily positions,
> dear Body, we thank thee
> and clothe thee.

> For being able to stand up to our daily positions,
> dear Body, we thank thee
> and feed thee.

> For being able to go forth in all forms and fancies,
> dear Body, we thank thee
> and exert thee.

(Voice):

> For being able to stand a great deal
> and sit it out to the end,
> dear Body, we thank thee and observe thee.

(Organ Fugue)
(Voice) Pater Noster:

> Our body, which is of earth,
> holied by thy shape.
> Thy beauty come,

thy acts be done,
on faith as they are given.

Give us each day our daily positions.
And forgive us our ineptitudes
as they do not forgive us.
Lead us not into ungracefulness
but deliver us from shamble.
For Thine is the standing, the sitting
and the lying
for ever and ever.

(Soprano) sings Pater Noster:

VI—for Erotica:

Gloria, with Musical Drug:
Mahalila, Mahasukha
Muladara, Sahasrara
Mudra, Shaki
Mahalila, Mahasukha

(Voice):

Body, which passeth all understanding,
keep your mind and flesh
in the union and love of life
now and forever hopeful.

VII—Finale: The Positions of the Gods

(Chorus) Kyrie:

Body, have beauty upon us.
Spirit, have beauty upon us.
Body, have beauty upon us.
Spirit, have beauty in us.
            Your body be with you.
            And with your spirit.

THIS IS IT (1971)

[In *Making Light of It* Broughton writes, "Watching my two-year-old son occupy the eternal moments of childhood play, I tried to capture his wonder with a little parable of Eden in our own backyard. Papa God in a treetop and Mother Earth inside a red ball speak the teachings of the world. David Myers' camera followed Baby Adam from the garden out to the streets of Mill Valley, while the ball chants its mantra: This is It..."]

This Is It (1971)
9 1/2 min. color 16mm sound
Directed and written by James Broughton.
Camera: David Myers.
Sound: Jerry Mueller.
Narration: James Broughton, George and Stefani Priest.
With [Broughton's son] Orion Broughton.

I

BALL: Om!

NARRATOR: In the beginning It was already there.
    And so was everything else.
    And everything was just the way It is.
    Then God came along.
    And God saw that It wasn't good enough.
    He said:

GOD: It needs something that looks more like me.
    (Thunderclap)
    Well, It will do for a start.
    And he shall have his dominion with everything as It is.

BALL: Om—Om!

GOD: Listen, Son!

ORION: Hi!

GOD: Keep your eye on the ball!
    Why do you think I made the world round?

BALL: Hmmmm.
    (Hums song)

GOD: That's more like It!

II

BALL: This is It.
    This is really It.
    This is all there is.
    And It's perfect as It is.

    There is nowhere to go
    but Here.
    There is nothing here
    but Now.
    There is nothing now
    but This.

    And this is It.
    This is really It.
    This is all there is.
    And It's perfect as It is.

III

GOD: So what is It?
    Is This It Here Now?

BALL: This Here Now It is.

GOD: Is Now It This Here?

BALL: Here It Now Is This.

GOD: Is It Here This Now?

BALL: Now Is Here This It.

GOD: Is This Now It Here?

BALL: This Now Here Is It.

GOD: You said It.

BALL: Om! Come on!
    Let go! Let's go!
    I am It
    and so are you!
    Omm... (into music)

IV

BALL: This is It
    and I am It
    and You are It
    and so is That
    and He is It
    and She is It
    and It is It
    and That is That.

    O It is This
    and It is Thus
    and It is Them
    and It is Us
    and It is Now
    and here It is
    and here We are
    so This is It.

DREAMWOOD (1972)

Dreamwood (1972)
46 min. color 16mm sound
Written and directed by James Broughton.
Camera: John Schofill and Fred Padula.
Editing: James Broughton and Kermit Sheets.
Sound: Jerry Mueller.
Music: Morton Subotnik
Cast: Henry Taylor and Margo St. James.

A NOTE ON *DREAMWOOD*

> "Somewhere there is a forest,
> somewhere at the center of the world
> there is a forest of the dream,
> a sacred wood, a grove of initiation.
> Somewhere there is what there has always been:
> the treasure hard to attain,
> the lair of the Great Goddess,
> the bed of the ultimate rapture."

Yes, somewhere (at the center of the world) there is an island called Animandra, or the Kingdom of Her. And somewhere in the wilds of Animandra there is a magic wood known as Broceliande, the Perilous Forest. Within this labyrinthine grove the dreamwood mysteries take place, the tests, the encounters, the rites of the Goddess in her many forms. Only a hero dares risk his life by entering this realm of the feminine powers. And most heroic is the poet, perhaps, guided as he is (and taunted) by that blessed damozel, his muse, whose name is Alchemina. Ordinary men remain safely outside in the dry meadows of their masculine games. But to the man who conquers his fear, persists in his quest and wins her favor, the Goddess of Dreamwood will reveal her greatest secret.

The subject of *Dreamwood* had obsessed me for years. I first conceived shaping it as a variation on the Theseus myth. But when the abandoned distillery I had planned to use as a setting was suddenly torn down, I restructured the material to fit the countryside near my home. We began filming on Bastille Day, 1970 in a forest near Muir Woods not far from the location site of *The Bed*. For 2 weeks we filmed every day; this included virtually all the footage on the island. *Dreamwood* could not have been made without support from the Guggenheim Foundation or without the devotion of my co-workers for whom it was often a rugged adventure. To John Schofill's camera eye the film owes its rigorous beauty. To Henry Taylor's protagonist the film owes it authentic commitment.

In August, Schofill had to leave for Chicago to take up duties at the School of the Art Institute. A month later I finished the opening sequence, the "call to adventure," with Fred Padula who had worked with me before on *The Golden Positions*. Kermit Sheets and I edited the film off and on all winter. In the summer of 1971 Jerry Mueller and I worked out the scoring of the sound. Morton Subotnik graciously gave me permission to use his music. At one point I wrote a long first-person narration, which finally I rejected. Just because one is a poet one does not have to verbalize. What I seek in cinema is a poetry of expressive image conveyed in metrical "vehicle for meanings," which hopefully may take us all into some vision of ecstasy.

DREAMWOOD: ORIGINAL SCRIPT

A man (we shall call him Janus) is discovered first in the "forest" of the city, despairing within its labyrinths, hence a crisis of his own identity.

He flees the city, pursued by Eumenides, passing its towers, its traffic; passing industrial embattlements, passing prisons, thick housing, freeways, waterside demolition and debris.

He also passes individual persons: a young woman with an infant, an old man lost in reveries, a drunk, an old lady (who offers him a drink), and a little boy who stops him and gives him a feather, and points the direction to go. Which is beyond all man-made structure and roadway. Into open fields. Toward the hills. And wild nature.

In a vast dry field he is crossing, Janus, hot and tired, is suddenly surprised by the appearance of a streetcar that stops near him, and the door opens. There is no one in it. He gets in. A naked woman materializes at the controls; smiles enigmatically; asks for the fare. He gives her the feather.

The streetcar travels across the landscape. He is the only passenger.

Janus is let out in a strange remote place: a dry valley with woods in the distance. The streetcar vanishes. A path leads down toward the woods.

But he is stopped abruptly from the descent by the appearance of what he takes to be a woman at a dressing table. She turns round and turns out to be bearded. Smiles enigmatically, coquettishly. He tries to get by her. She waylays him with enticements, grotesque flirtation, which leads into a struggle that is half erotic and half a fight for his life.

Ultimately Janus must surrender to her, acknowledge her power; otherwise he will not be allowed to proceed. When he does, the bearded lady transforms: becomes very gentle, even genteel and helpful. Takes him to the mirror at her table; makes him look in it: a confrontation.

In the mirror he sees behind him many mysterious figures in a landscape, satyrs, nymphs, an old crone, a woman in black, devils. And his own image is black.

When he turns around to behold the reality, there is only the bare landscape.

Also, turning around again, he discovers the Lady has vanished, with her dressing table. There is no one around. Until he sees down the trail a large antique doll dressed in Victorian clothes; and opposite it, further on, a live Herm, smiling, with erect penis.

Beyond these he sees a little girl beckoning him to follow and running on till she disappears by the woods.

Following the direction of the little girl, he heads for the forest. Coming toward him (from the forest) is a sage, with bow and arrow, grinning, shooting arrows straight up into the air to see if he can hit himself on the head.

Janus cannot find the entrance into the forest; it is impenetrable with bramble. The little girl he sees again, up ahead, running.

Finally he comes to the entrance to the forest, where a fallen tree is like a gate. In this tree is the "gatekeeper": a nun in black. She will not let him enter until he has taken down his pants and shown her his private parts. She smiles; with conditional permission. Then she disrobes, and flings her habit over his head.

When the blackness lifts he is inside the forest; just inside the "gate." There is a sense of terrifying beauty; a temple of tree-trunks, flickering light, strange sounds. He thinks he sees dryads in the trees; women's hair in the branches; faces in the knotholes.

First encounter: Artemis bathing.

Janus spies her through a thicket; hearing the sound of the brook, and her splashing. She has two attendants, pouring water from urns over her limbs. Loveliness of the bath, and the virgin goddess never seen by man. The action is ritualized and pure.

When discovered, Artemis is furious. Turns her hounds upon him. He flees.

Each time, after each encounter, he finds himself (or comes to) outside of the woods: in the sunlit world, the world of the open field where he will see visions of masculine mysteries: young bucks leaping about; a woodcutter; a man carrying a trunk; the tattooed man; Priapus and the phallic rites; etc. As well as a confrontation with vultures, with snakes, with rusted machinery and the like.

Second encounter:

He finds the entrance to the forest again. This time there is an older woman, very ceremonious, robed. Who grabs his arm, and draws blood with a knife. Smiles and disappears.

He climbs through the gate.

He proceeds to a clearing, which feels particularly intense, where he pauses in profound reverie. Offers some of his blood.

Looking up, he sees suddenly two lovely twin girls voluptuously beckoning to him. They disappear, and appear again. At length they turn and passionately attack him, and try to tickle him to death.

In the exhaustion of sexuality turned to giggling absurdity, again he finds himself outside the forest.

Third encounter:

He enters the wood a different way, through a narrow thicket.

Circe, as a fortune teller. Lithe, wide-eyed, subtle, frightening. With a "magic table" of changing colors. Flinging cards of all kinds, stones, coins. Then putting everything in a cauldron. She splashes the contents in his face. He is turned into a goat, which she rides.

Fourth encounter:

A black woman wearing red beads, moving in slow motion. Lilith. And the rites of stupor and intoxication madness. With attendants. She gives him liquors to drink, while caressing him, undressing him. And giving him her snakes to kiss.

Delirium. Unconsciousness.

Fifth encounter:

Hecate. The jaws of death. Turned to stone. Devoured.

She is the most frightening, the ultimate hag. And this is the supreme test. He is able to embrace her.

This time he is not outside the forest. He is still within. And in an open glade of a very special feeling, the light trembling. He is awed. He feels the presence of the great goddess herself.

He throws himself down upon the earth, seeking its renewal. Something comes back to him from within it. He rises, aware of the imminence of the great initiation ritual. He slowly disrobes. He makes ritual offering of his body: urine, and feces, spittle, snot, earwax, and blood. Then he goes in the stream to cleanse himself in purification. (The attendants of Artemis stand by to bathe him.)

Returning to the magic circle, he finds two slugs gratefully devouring his shit. And that the place is now marked off in a circle: the natural bed of the goddess.

Like a man approaching the bed of his unknown bride, Janus with awe climbs into the circle of the earth; begins wooing the earth, caressing, making love to Her, of all women, receptive, elusive, enticing, all-embracing. His sense of union grows. He has ecstatic orgasm with Her: he "dies" again in this ecstasy of seeding his own rebirth.

And then, miraculously, he feels the sun upon his back (warmth, as well, from behind); feels himself enclosed between Great Mother and

Great Father, like a new seed, a new creature.

And this experience is so real that it is as if there were a glorious glowing woman beneath him and a strong warm man behind him, filling him with seeds of the sun.

When this experience of union passes, he turns and slowly rises, finding himself in a totally different place—between forest and meadow. And he is radiant in the sunlight. And as he stands we can see that within him is the body of a woman fully contained and at peace.

Standing fully erect, with this inner living miracle contained inside him, he opens out his arms.

This image of union and unity achieved is seen, with behind it in a sequence a running back of the landscapes through which he has come, back to the city, and ultimately to the ocean—taking the resolution back into the world from which he came.

HIGH KUKUS (1973)

High Kukus (19973)
3 min. 16 mm
Directed by James Broughton.
Written by James Broughton.
Camera: H.E. Jenkins II.
Sound mix: John Cavala.

Note: All but two of the high kukus spoken on the sound track were especially written for the film.

This is my most Zen film, a visualization of the Zen dictum of "sitting quietly, doing nothing" being present in the Now of the moment. Or, as I put it in my poem "The Birds of America": "to simply sit about and scratch/and watch what's going on." The film is also an homage to my favorite Japanese poet, Basho, and particularly to his famous haiku about the frog jumping into the pond. Not being Japanese myself I have created my own verse form in the terse style; and much more anthropomorphic in its content than Basho would ever allow, although relevant to Chuan-Tzu's fable-making perhaps. Example:

> I have no meaning,
> Said the Film,
> I just unreel myself.

[Descriptions of subsequent Broughton films appear in *Making Light of It*. Here are a few excerpts:]

TESTAMENT (1974) 20 minutes

In 1972 I was invited to present a speech at the opening of the new county library in the town of Modesto, California. The librarian wanted an inaugural address by an author who had been born in the town. I was the only candidate they could unearth. When I explained to my class in Film Directing at San Francisco State University that I would be unable to meet them on the day of the event, they proposed staging a "homecoming" parade for me through the streets of the town. From the footage of that colorful occasion, I spun what I thought would be my final film: a self-portrait bouncing me from my babyhood to my imagined death. To summarize the quest for erotic transcendence that animated all my cinema I mixed film clips, still photos and stages scenes. I was assisted at the camera by an ingratiating redhead named H. Edgar Jenkins, who had filmed the Modesto parade in slow motion. At the film's beginning I am seen rocking in a chair by the Pacific Ocean, questioning my life:

> I asked the Sea how deep things are.
> O, said She, that depends upon
> how far you want to go.

The Water Circle, an homage to Lao-tsu, followed in 1975 and *Erogeny* in 1976: "The major technical hurdle [of *Erogeny*] was finding persons in Pittsburgh willing to take off their clothes.' *Together* (1976) was the first of Broughton's collaborations with Joel Singer—a collaboration, that would continue until the end of Broughton's life. *Windowmobile*, "a mobile-home movie," followed in 1977, as did *Song of the Godbody*. In 1979 Broughton and Singer made *Hermes Bird*: "To watch the subtle pulsations of a penis growing erect I filmed in extreme slow motion.

Access to one of the official cameras used to photograph the atomic bomb explosions in the South Pacific allowed me to capture the slowest ascension of a penis that has ever been seen." In 1981 came *The Gardner of Eden*: "In 1980 Joel and I lived on a rubber plantation on the island of Sri Lanka. This vernal paradise belonged to the tallest man on the island who was also its most famous horticulturist. I pictured him as God trying to keep an eye on the flowering proliferation of his world." *Shaman Psalm*, a reading of Broughton's "anti-war canticle," followed in 1981 and *Devotions* in 1983: "Joel and I set out to show some of the ways that men can enjoy one another without resorting to insult or aggression. We filmed forty-five couples in a variety of locations from Seattle to San Diego." *Scattered Remains* was James Broughton's last film:

SCATTERED REMAINS (1988) 14 minutes

In 1988 when the San Francisco International Film Festival planned to honor me with a tribute to my forty years of filmmaking, I thought it apropos to prepare a new work for the occasion. Joel proposed making yet another portrait of me, this time his "Portrait of the Poet as James Broughton." He devised a dozen techniques to enliven my reading of a dozen poems. The last of these is, "I hear the happy sound of one hand clapping/all the way to Buddha land." In the final image clowns first seen on a beach at the beginning reappear transformed into Pan and Hermes dancing away toward the sea.

James Broughton's films are available on 16mm from Canyon Cinema, 2325 Third Street, San Francisco, CA 94107 and on video cassette and DVD from Facets, 1517 West Fullerton Avenue, Chicago, IL 60614.

SUPERIOR WACKINESS

High Kukus, Alan Watts, and Buddha Land

SUPERIOR WACKINESS : HIGH KUKUS, ALAN WATTS, AND BUDDHA LAND

Throughout his life, Broughton delighted in friendship and was himself a wonderful friend. His involvement with Zen Buddhism included a personal involvement with Alan Watts, a scholar of Eastern religions whose book *This Is It* gave the poet the title of a film and some delightful poems. In *Coming Unbuttoned* Broughton writes that "Alan admitted he cherished metaphysical nonsense as a key to the Infinite.... [His] playfulness relieved the solemnity of Jungian symbolizing. He took me through non-symbolic realms of philosophy into the superior wackiness of Zen and the sunlit moments of Taoism. I hung out with him to keep my soul in balance, sat in on his lectures, made up verses to amuse him. He adopted me as the jester poet of his private court." One of Watts' close friends, poet Elsa Gidlow, accused Broughton of making fun of Watts in the verses he composes: "Alan retaliated that I was the one person who really caught on to his crazy wisdom." In his introduction to the 1968 Jargon Society Rainbow Edition of *High Kukus*, Alan Watts wrote:

> James Broughton's *High Kukus* are a slightly zany, or cuckoo, combination of both [haiku and senryu, the latter a more vulgar form of haiku, usually ribald or humorous] with the extra special quality of being "high" in two senses, of which the first is that they are often metaphysical, and the second that they are "high" as the adjective is now vulgarly used to denote a peculiar state of consciousness in which one is keenly aware of what Gerald Heard called the "meta-comedy" of things.
>
> G.K. Chesterton once observed that when a typesetter substitutes "comic" for "cosmic" he is not really too much in

error…. The point is that one trembles with anxiety in feeling that being is ever in danger of lapsing into permanent non-being. But one trembles with laughter (at oneself) when it is realized that non-being implies being just as much as the reverse. For the cosmos is a game of hide-and-seek.

To understand this is to understand meta-comedy…. In the contemplation of lofty themes most people are serious, though not always sincere. Broughton, however, is always sincere but hardly ever serious.

Indeed, seriousness is a questionable virtue: it is gravity rather than levity, and it was … that devout Catholic, Chesterton, who maintained that the angels fly because they take themselves lightly. And, in company with the angels, Broughton laughs with God rather than at him.

HIGH KUKUS

I have no desire to move about,
said the Tree,
I'm very attached to my roots.

*

They keep cutting me off,
said the Whisker,
but that will never stop me.

*

You may have had some hard knocks,
said the Pebble,
but I've been kicked around all my life.

*

There's nothing I like better,
said the Sun,
than throwing some light on the subject.

*

You always think I'm greener elsewhere,
said the Grass.
Well, sometimes I am.

*

That's just your opinion,
said the Pterodactyl,
I think I'm gorgeous.

*

I'm madly in love with a frog,
said the Goat,
but she has a crazy idea that it won't work out.

*

Before swallowing me whole,
said the Panacea,
see if your solution doesn't need shaking up.

*

To think of ending my days covered with catsup,
said the Bull,
makes me see red.

*

A little bird told me,
said the Eagle,
and then I ate him.

*

I admit it,
said the Rat,
I'm as much of a rat as the next fellow.

*

Sometimes,
said the Telephone,
I can scarcely believe my ears.

*

I may be infecting the whole body,
said the Head,
but they'll never amputate me.

*

I'm hungry,
said the Bulldozer,
I want a hillburger for lunch.

*

There will be time,
said the Grandfather Clock,
for whatever there will be time for.

*

Of course I'm infinite,
said the Grain of Sand,
but what's the rest of this beach doing here?

*

I need something to pick me up,
said the Sweet Pea,
I'm dying on the vine.

*

I wish these damn angels would get their feet off my
    head,
said the Pin,
I've got work to do.

*

Get out of here!
said the Mouth to the Foot,
And with that big shoe on too!
*

We may look weird,
said the Platypus to his wife,
but we have each other.
*

I don't know what the left is doing,
said the Right Hand,
but it looks fascinating.
*

There might be someone else inside you,
said the Mirror,
beside you.
*

When things get too tight for me,
said the Snake,
I just slip into some skin more comfortable.
*

There's practically nothing,
said the Eraser,
that ever comes out perfectly.
*

There are two sides to everything,
said the Coin.
John is a saint and John is a toilet.
*

Going around in theological circles,
said the Dove,
God must get very dizzy.
*

When I gave up trying to understand,
said the Camel's Eye to the Needle,
then I began to get the point.

*

It's quite easy to be enlightened,
said the Lamp,
once you get turned on,

*

If you take one thing at a time,
said the Stepping Stone,
you can endure anything.

*

Nothing is nicer than letting go,
said the Leaf,
when that's the only thing to do.

*

I can't help playing around,
said the Wind,
I'm just naturally impulsive.

*

What I am sometimes is never always clear,
said the Pond,
What I am always is never clear all the time.

*

Never expect anything,
said the Tadpole,
and everything will surprise you.

*

I love candlelight,
said the Moth,
It makes suicide more romantic.

*

It makes a terrible mess,
said the Cup,
but I love running over.

*

Anyway you look at it,
said the Camera,
this is the way it is.

*

I have no meaning,
said the Film,
I just unreel myself.
*

You can always count on me in a pinch,
said the Penis,
I've gotten out of many a tight spot.
*

You can't get around me easily,
said the Vicious Circle,
I'm one turning point after another.
*

I don't know where I'm heading,
said the Rolling Stone,
but it's uphill all the way.
*

Wherever you make your home,
said the Waterbug,
is the center of the world.
*

I'd love a new outfit,
said the Attitude,
but I can't get out of this old habit.
*

Don't worry,
said the Caterpillar,
we'll all come out beautifully in the end.
*

Isn't it perverse?
said the Cradle to the Hearse,
Things are getting better and things are getting
worse.

FORGET-ME-NOTS FOR ALAN WATTS
On his Fiftieth Birthday

Does anyone know the true wherefores and whats
of this singular person called Alan Watts?

Does he get his ideas for his seminar talks
by going on long cross-country walks, or trots,
Mr. Alan Watts?

When he writes out a chapter to confound the wise
does he cross all his T's and finish his I's with dots,
does Alan Watts?

Does he do his thinking in pontifical hats?
Does he sleep on a bed or on Japanese mats, or on cots,
this Alan Watts?

Can he write his calligraphy concisely clear
without any smudge, any speck or smear, or blots,
can Alan Watts?

Does he get his kicks by the clear blue waves
or by prowling about in dark green caves, or in grots,
the Alan of Watts?

When he grows inspired with brilliant notions
does he dance about in primitive motions, or gavottes,
Dr. Alan Watts?

Does he practice sex magic in sacred rivers?
Do beautiful women give him the shivers, or the hots?
O Alan Watts!

Is it true that at birth he gave a great shout
and said, I've already figured life out in my thoughts,
said Baby Watts?

Did he also remark to his parents from the crib,
Your concept of truth is a childish fib, you clots,
said Little Watts?

And when he had made all his family skittish
did he then upset the rest of the British, including the Scots,
did Alan Watts?

Was it in America, and do you know when
that he put down Jesus and took up Zen, and other whatnots,
the Reverend Watts?

Is he now quite content with his own dominion?
Does he care not a fig for public opinion, or lots,
does Alan Watts?

Is it true that he thrives on exotic drugs
which he keeps in barrels, trunks and jugs, and in pots,
this Alan Watts?

Though it's said that he breakfasts on LSD,
does he swallow the stuff in his morning tea, or in shots?
Why, Alan Watts!

When he gives a lecture for all to hear
does he leave his audience perfectly clear, or in knots,
Professor Watts?

Though much we'll never know of this remarkable man,
let us toast him tonight for his fifty-year span, like sots!
Hail, Alan Watts!

6 January 1965

THOSE OLD ZEN BLUES
or, AFTER THE SEMINAR

It's not because it is.
It's not because it isn't.
It is because it is
because it's not at all.

In Zen you can't yen for anything
since nothing can be had.
When nothing is real in reality
nothing is good or bad.

There's nothing in heaven, nothing in hell,
and nothing is what I am.
Something is where it always was
but it doesn't give a damn.

It's not because it is.
It is because it isn't.
It isn't because it's not.
It's not because at all.

The life I think I ought to live
is just a thought in my head.
I ought to throw my thoughts away
and believe in nothing instead.

There's nothing where I start from
and nothing I comprehend.
Unless I get enlightenment
I'll be nothing in the end.

It isn't there because it's there.
It's there because it isn't.
It's where it is because it is
and not because it isn't.

BUDDHA LAND
(A Zen Spiritual)

I hear the happy sound of
one hand clapping
that old hand clapping
that big hand clapping—
I hear the happy sound of
one hand clapping
all the way to Buddha Land.

     Koan Baby, don't you cry, don't you cry!
     Koan Baby, don't you cry!

There's a great big emptiness
waiting for everyone
open to everyone
big enough for everyone—
A great big emptiness
waiting for everyone
when you get to Buddha Land.

     Koan Baby, don't you cry, don't you cry!
     Koan Baby, don't you cry!

There's a big bodhisattva
dishing out enlightenment
serving up enlightenment
feeding you enlightenment—
A big bodhisattva
dishing out enlightenment
when you get to Buddha Land.

     Koan Baby, don't you cry, don't you cry!
     Koan Baby, don't you cry!

EXCERPTS FROM A JOURNAL

EXCERPTS FROM A JOURNAL

This is a selection from an unpublished journal written in 1979. Broughton's memoir, *Coming Unbuttoned*, describes his mental state four years earlier, when he had reached the age of sixty-two. Convinced by friends and his Jungian analysis that marriage would be a good thing for him, he had married Suzanna Hart in 1962 and raised a family. But by 1975 both his marriage and his work had reached a state of crisis:

> I thought I had everything I had to say, except perhaps for some graceful farewell. Besides, my sagging energies were reflected in my home life. In the marriage bed I had encountered the consternation of impotence. Suzanna's resentment of this took an inevitable turn: she asked me to move out of our bedroom and sleep in my studio.

Broughton's work at all periods contains individual embodiments of energy, savior figures, often (though not always) conceived of as male. These figures are associated with fire (warmth and light) as well as with film. The earliest is "Hermy," with his "pulsing hot sparkler" and his "throbbing wand." In Broughton's moment of need, Hermy appeared again in the person of a twenty-five-year-old Canadian film student named Joel Singer. As Broughton tells the story in his poem, "Wondrous the Merge" (1982), he protested that a serious relationship with Singer was "preposterous.... I have a wife in the suburbs / I have mortgages

children in-laws/ and a position in the community." Singer
     dismissed my rebuffs and ultimatums
     He scoffed at suggestions of disaster
     He insisted he had been given authority
     to provide my future happiness
     Was it possible he had been sent
     from some utopian headquarters?

Broughton married Joel Singer on Christmas Eve, 1976. Though "cinematic opponents"—"I relished slow motion effects" while "Joel's passion was speedy single framing"—their relationship remained at the heart of the rest of his life's work. This journal documents their first lengthy trip together: "our three week honeymoony voyage." The trip (which included Guam, Hong Kong, Singapore, Bali —"a land of androgynes"—Java and Sri Lanka) comes at a moment in which Broughton is still reeling from the effects of his extraordinary personal transformation. The journal begins a week before his sixty-sixth birthday. He is eager "to be free of the shore, of all the old responsibilities," to "connect to what precedes not only the U.S., but precedes Europe as well":

    Last night Joel Singer asked me if there was any sexually free society in the world, & was perhaps San Francisco the most liberated place.... A crucial question. Is all the world morally repressed by its official religions? All of them— Islam, Christianity, Hinduism, Judaism, Buddhism—all are puritanically afraid of love & discourage passion. All of them are in business to control instincts. For me this is a big challenge. I know that I am not the wrong one in knowing that the world has arranged it all wrong. It does have to be done anew and started fresh: a complete revolution back to the beginning. Which is why we are here visiting Edens.

Nov 3, 1979. At sea.

On the Pacific aboard SS President Van Buren—American
President Lines,
Cabin 1
Six a.m. the morning after sailing from Oakland.

What an exhilaration,
What a wrench.
And again, after so many years, to be on shipboard rolling
on the waves—
at last at last!
The weeks of preparation and waiting are over, the
anxiety, the eagerness to be free of the shore, of all the old
responsibilities.

Roy and Jac brought us to Oakland to the ship, and left us
a bon voyage basket of goodies. We had a bottle of champagne
in the parlor of our suite. How tender and dear Roy is, what
elegance of feeling! I love him deeply.
They served dinner at 5 p.m.
Unbelievably ordinary.
After that a company cocktail party. We sailed at 8.
Magical passing under the bridges & past San Francisco
lights out into the Pacific—out into the currents of the ocean.
I kept waking during the night catching the rhythms of
the ship's toss.
It is beautiful and vast upon the sea. Already what is left
behind seems petty. I am grateful beyond measure to be able
to leave the U.S. behind for a time. Specifically our California
life. Specifically the proximity of [my wife] Suzanna. There
are blessings upon this voyage & this adventure. It acts like a
rebirthing—a return to the primeval waters, to the source, to
the ancient peoples & civilizations. Renewal. Connect to what
precedes not only the U.S., but precedes Europe as well.

After noon.

The ship rolls & tosses in heavy deep-blue seas: it is a rite of passage. I feel my mind emptying of old garbage, of fret & fuss, & bilge of yakyak & worry. It is letting go. It is shedding. I am on the edge of queasy. But sharpening. I have been reading the *Gay Sunshine* interviews to determine my own mythography for mine.

Androgyne as what it means to me, needs redefining. Or a new word. HeShe? I am talking of a condition beyond the opposites, not of an alteration between them. I don't mean only bisexuality. I mean 'thrust and surrender' go together. The enlightened man is he who experiences both: penetrating and being penetrated, until he himself richly penetrant: a penetrating being penetrated with love, penetrating into all the reaches of the soul.

It is soul I mean when I speak of androgyne. For such is the nature of soul, such its context.

I have read the whole volume of *Gay Sunshine* interviews. The majority have no vision. And less faith. No delight in the soul, no hope for mankind.

Acknowledge that I am most enchanted by the bodies of men & the psyches of men, and the aromas of men. That I have always had much womanness in me—identification with the female mystique, with her way of looking to the man with adoration and desire, eager to surrender to him, be upheld and penetrated, be fondled and indulged. This desire has been gratified in Joel. And my life redeemed.

I want to give every man a dynamic divinity
that he knows
that he feels
that he relishes
I want every man to enjoy his divines.

Feeling/Feeling experience—this I hope men will open for themselves.

November 4

The sea straightens out a bit this morning after yesterday's bumps. The moon was full. We were the only ones on deck to see it. There was a John Wayne movie on the video. The Purser has an enormous pot belly and loves to talk. Already the monotony begins: the hum of the unceasing movement across the vast sea.

November 5 6 a.m.

I had a long sleepless dreaming: not getting anywhere, not reaching the destination, constantly sidetracked. There was no room for us on the bus, we walked behind it with some others, until the bus driver stalled it under a tree & climbed out to go into a local marketplace. We were always trying to find out when we might leave, where we might get to, but there were new snags and delays—like the huge airplanes flying very low, made in long sections that could fit together like 4 or 6 ordinary jet bodies: were they going to a war? Were they readying to attack us?

It seemed ultimately that one should abandon all hope of getting to there. Whereas, in actuality, we move ahead across the Pacific, on and on, through sun and shower and moon and cloud. Someone has been an albatross.

The captain gave a party last night: cocktails & dinner with wine. We have 4 Canadians, 3 of them naturalized Britons. An elderly couple from Maine whose anthropological son teaches in eastern Australia & is married to a Malaysian Chinese from Kuala Lumpur; they are going to Australia for Christmas, & going fishing in New Zealand. There are three single ladies and one single gentleman, and ourselves.

Our dining steward is amazingly inept. I like the parlor of our suite. Truly private. I am beginning to feel more alert. The sea is wondrous. Am I never to 'get there'? Is it that there is nowhere or nothing to get to? Be not anxious! The Guardians are running the ship, they are working out the itinerary.

November 6

By now the sea has leveled off into magic blue, the horizons surround, the skies are densely clear, the air is warming.

I had a good energy yesterday: after having dragged around the manuscripts for years, I typed into shape a first draft of *Graffiti for the Johns of Heaven.* I have not had such pleasure in concentration for a long time. I like the augury: that this shall mark a creative time.

I begin to get the rhythm of these days and go with them: it opens exhilarance. It is 6 a.m. & I am sitting on deck in a sun-rising breeziness.

Joel has had more seasickness to cope with: a slow adjusting to the element and the spacious-surround enclosure that shipboard is—all this space around our confinement. He begins to look more like himself, he surrenders his pallor. He is wonderfully loving. I count myself supremely blessed to enjoy such wedding and devotion. Through him I am loved by the true & real one, by the gods of my faith, & by all the fair men in the world. What sweeter fulfillment?

November 7

Yesterday afternoon, when I was typing out *Androgyne* material, the sea worsened & stormed, by dinnertime we had taken a Dramamine, & after dinner no one was up to playing the announced Bingo. J & I spent the evening in our bunks reading, it was too rocky to sit up.

How easy it could be to see this traverse as an ordeal: when O when will the winds ever die? But the truth of the matter is: we are going for the journey, not the destination. I asked Joel why are we on this trip?

He said: So that you can write a masterpiece.

Me: Oh. I had forgotten.

So I had a long dream of having to find the young persons, including ones like my children, who had to be paid what was owed them. It was a complicated search through unnamed villages. And payment could only be made piecemeal. Please, sir, no need to feel guilty.

November 8

We become more & more part of this floating island, & more & more in timelessness. No news, no interruptions, inured in movement with the sea. A 'family' (of distant cousins) develops.

We toured the bridge yesterday and examined the instruments and charts. We played Scrabble at the cocktail hour. A terrible move, *Mandingo*.

We are trying to rewrite the *Gay Sunshine* interview. There will be no tomorrow. We cross directly into November 10 over the imaginary threshold of the dateline.

There is no Friday November 9th out here on the middle of the water. It is now [his birthday] November 10, 1979, for we have crossed the international dateline. We are somewhere near the Marianas. White birds zoom over the big swells this morning & the ship moves on long slow rolls. It is odd to think that this is my 66th birthday: surrounded by water, unconnected to land, between continents, between worlds. An apt place for a Scorpio?

November 11

It is still stormy. High long rollers keeping us on the constant uneven. Rain. There was no sun yesterday. Amusement: what I had expected to be my birthday 'party' last evening turned out to be a Captain's party for crossing the dateline. I had a cake at the end of the meal. But no one even said Happy Birthday. Nor congratulated me. So much for our little egos.

We had a picnic at lunch time, on the goodies Roy & Jac gave us in a basket when we sailed: Brie, pate, pickled corn, apples, & Beaujolais. We had a bottle of Kornell before the cocktail time. I was happiest in that time, & being loved by my loved one.

It has been a week on board. Still it feels like a serious rite of passage. And an endurance. I have to remind myself that Azoth [Alchemy: the metal mercury; quicksilver; the Roman god Mercury is the equivalent to the Greek god Hermes—ed.]

is at the helm, and that we shall not fall off the edge of the world.

November 13

Calm seas, benign skies, mellow motion, sunshine & warmth. Ripest blue of the water flying fish & an odd bird—a night of incredible stars—a sunrise just now I witnessed from the bridge deck: a total 360 degrees holy delicacy, God in his glory all around.

One is grateful to be 'swimming' in utterly different latitudes just rolling along, going with it, going nowhere going anywhere.

On the other hand last night I had dreams that disturbed and woke me. First: was Suzanna, & my having to call her on the phone & try to explain where I was setting out for & why I had to go. And I could not make it clear, I could not convince her, I could not present a good argument, I met only resistance & resentment & what became hostility & denunciation and ultimately impenetrable obstacle. This was so strong that I could not shake it when awake. I was like one condemned & incarcerated & cornered.

Then when sleep came again it seemed I spent the rest of the night forced to cope with and evaluate complex charts that showed how much we would all be indebted in the future. It was difficult work. The prices were in huge figures & fat files. I was consistently scolded for not applying myself more assiduously. It certainly had to do with expected difficulties.

I don't know causes for these nightmarish fantasies, which ultimately got me out of bed before dawn. Unless it be as Opposite reacting to the euphoria of being loved & beautifully fucked & joyful chockablock with affectionateness. Plus asseverating outrageous orgasmanism for *Gay Sunshine* interview. Are these threats like retribution fears?

On conscious level I am aware of 'escaping' Suzanna on this voyage, & also responsibilities of the future. That's just the crux perhaps: that I am to 'go beyond' such a horizon, and accept instead the Life of the Erotic Poet full-tilt & unquestioning. I have nothing to fear from S. except my fear of her. And the factualities of the future will occur in any case.

> Kiss my heart
> Suck on my heart
> O love hungry one
> Kiss my heart
> Feed on my heart
> Take all the nourishment my heart has to give
> Feed on my in your own heart
> Feed your heart with mine
> Take transfusion
> from heart to heart
> direct.
> Beloved fills me with the flowers of his beauty
> His ardor intensifies my own
> He is taking me to the place for my madness to glow
> He is taking me out from under all I do not need.
> He is the tending gardener of my poetree
> He will bring it into cultivation
> He will watch it burst with fruit.
> "I want you to live your poetry", he said
> "I want you to live all you imagine" he said
> "That is why we are on this trip."
> He fills me with the passionate energy in his body
> He gives it all to me
> He adores my soul
> He caresses my soul
> He explodes my soul
> I am rolling in ecstasy with his blessing

Shaman Psalm / Erogeny

SHAMAN PSALM / EROGENY

With the publication of *Graffiti for the Johns of Heaven* (1982), *Ecstasies* (1983) and *A to Z: 26 Sermonettes* (1986), James Broughton begins to emerge not only as an artist but as a shaman, a prophet—though, typically, an extraordinarily light-hearted one:

HERE COMES YOUR MESSIAH

Hello again This is your overhead operator
I am the big message at the end of your beep
If I plug you in   will you return my call?

It is one of his many transformations. The role of "prophet" marks the appearance of individuation's "Great Man": partially parodied in his film, *Testament* (1974), it now manifests as a genuine aspect of Broughton's own personality. The film *Shaman Psalm* appeared in 1981. In it, a very serious Broughton—a far cry from the comic, self-pitying, boyish Broughton of 1950's *Adventures of Jimmy*—is seen reciting a poem "pleading for a world of peace-loving comrades." "Shocked by a century of ceaseless war-making," Broughton writes in Making Light of It, "I wrote a poem pleading for a world of peace-loving comrades. When we attended a large men's gathering in Colorado Joel photographed random scenes of the group activity. These we later organized into a flow of images to accompany my reading of the antiwar canticle..."

In a 1987 interview with Joseph W. Bean (*The Advocate,* Issue 486) Broughton asserted that "More and more I have come to feel that those of us who are working for consciousness—not all gay men, certainly—have a shaman role":

[Broughton explains] that, like the shamans of many earlier cultures, gay men are the people in the modern world who can step outside the usual responsibilities and controlling forces —"the breeder game"— and separate themselves from the collective values...

What Broughton calls 'Divine Androgynes" are the rarest and most important individuals of our time, he explains. They are the gayest possible people but, by definition, are not necessarily homosexual. Broughton is adamant about the fact that gaiety is not an exclusively homosexual territory. "I don't make that distinction. Quite the contrary, I think it's very possible for heterosexuals, if they will understand, if they will develop in themselves the other side that can make this happen for them. I had many classmates who were potential dancers in the world, but then they got trapped in the breeding game. They became dedicated to those values and began to live for the children and didn't develop themselves. It's better if they're bisexual because this way, in relation to another man, a man can relate to his own nature better."

In Broughton's early work, children are victimized by adults. Here, in the world of "the breeding game," "to live for the children" is to err. In a late interview he remarked, "You must take care of your inner child all your life. That's the one to raise…"

James Broughton wrote a great many explicitly homoerotic love poems. His term "erogeny"—also the title of a film (1976)—is perhaps meant to counter terms like "misogyny," which involve hatred ("miso-"). The O.E.D. gives "erogenic": "That gives rise to sexual desire." Though Broughton's poems are often addressed specifically, the lover in them, especially in the later work, tends to become identical with God. "God Is My Beloved" is an example of what the poet called "mash notes to God," though he always remained capable of effusions like:

> Nipples and cocks
> nipples and cocks
> Nothing tickles the palate like
> nipples and cocks…
>
> No need to be fancy
> or unorthodox
> Just try a plain diet of
> nipples and cocks

Broughton put it graphically in Graffiti for the *Johns of Heaven:* "God and fuck belong together."

SHAMAN PSALM

Listen   Brothers   Listen
The alarms are on fire
The oracles are strangled
Hear the pious vultures
condemning your existence
Hear the greedy warheads
Calling for your death
Quick while there's time
Take heed   Take heart
Claim your innocence
Proclaim your fellowship
Preach to each other
Connect one another
and hold

Rescue your lifeline
Defy the destroyers
Defy the fat vandals
They call for a nation
of castrated bigots
They promise a reward
of disaster and shame
Defy them   Deny them
Quick while there's hope
Renovate man
Insist on your brotherhood
Insist on humanity
Love one another
and live

Release your mind from
the handcuffs of guilt
Take off your blinders
Focus your insight
Take off the bandages

that infect your fears
See your wounds heal when
you know your birthright
Men are not foes
Man are born loving
welcome being tingled by
the touch of devotion
Honor one another
or lose
Come Brothers Waken
Uproot hostility
Root out the hypocrites
Warm up your phoenix
to arouse a new era
Disarm the cutthroats
Sever the loggerheads
Offset the history
of torment and curse
Man is the species
endangered by man
Quick while there's time
Abandon your rivalries
or mourn

Come forth unabashed
Come out unbuttoned
Bury belligerence
Resurrect frolic
Only through body can
you clasp the divine
Only through body can
you dance with the god
In every man's hand
the gift of compassion
In every man's hand
the beloved connection
Trust one another
or drown

Banish animosity
Summon endearment
You are kindred to
each one you greet
each one you deal with
crossing the world
Salute the love ability
in all those you meet
Elicit the beauty that
hides in all flesh
Let freedom of feeling
liberate mankind
Love one another
at last

Hold nothing back
Hold nothing in
Romp and commingle
out in the open
Parade your peculiar
Shine your monkey
Rout the sourpuss
Outrage the prig
Quick while there's room
revel in foolhardy
Keep fancies tickled
Grow fond of caress
Go forthright together
or fail

Affirm your affection
Be laughing in wisdom
You are a miracle
dismissed as a moron
You are a godbody
avoiding holiness
Claim your dimension
Insist on redemption

Love between men will
anachronize war
bring joy into office
and erogenate peace
Accept one another
and win

Relish new comrades
Freshen new dreams
Speak from the heart
Sing from the phallus
Keep holy bounce in
your intimate ballgames
Sexual fervor can
leap over galaxy
outburst the sun
football the moon
Give way to love
Give love its way
Ripen one another
or rot

Extend your vision
Stretch your exuberance
Offer your body to
the risk of delight
where soul can run naked
spirit jump high
Taste the divine on
the lips of lover
Savor the divine on
the thigh of friend
Treasure the divinity
that ignites the orgasm
Surprise the eagles
and soar

Let the weapons rust
Let the powers crumble
Open your fists
into embraces
Open your armslength
into loving circles
Be champions of hug
Be warriors of kiss
Prove in beatitude
a new breed of man
Prove that comradeship
is the crown of the gods
Cherish one another
and thrive

Listen Brothers Listen
The alarms are too late
This is the hour for
amorous revolt
Dare to take hold
Dare to take over
Be heroes of harmony
in bedfellow bliss
Man must love man
or war is forever
Outnumber the hawks
Outdistance the angels
Love one another
Or die

EROGENY

Reach
      Touch
            Discover

We are hemispheres
      ebbing and flowing
We are continents
          meeting

Discover
     my oases
         explore me

I am
     a terrain of
     meadows and prairies
         moors   mesas
hillocks   ravines   and wild grasses
Approach
     Reach
         Touch me

Visit my archipelagos
     my tropics
         my equator
Share your shoreline
        with my peninsulas
     my coves   channels
        and deep lagoons

Graze gently
          my pastures   my pathways
Learn
          my landmarks
My topography leads to
                    uncharted regions
          savannas   sierras
          dunes   and swamps   and
                    hidden caves

I am
          an alluvial horizon
I am
          an aromatic wilderness
                    of thickets
and vines and trailing branches
          mosses   and ferns
                    and herbal grottoes

I exude
          oils   attars   resin
                    seedpods   pollen
          and spicy fruits

Touch
          Come near
                    Explore
this torrid geology

Out of fossil and clay
          marrow and lavaflow
our volcanic latitudes
          smolder
                    swelter

our landmasses
               shift
our mudpots and fumaroles
            craters and geysers
quake
         shiver
                 erupt

From tundra to jungle
from summit to riverrun
         in heatwave
                 in downpour
I am
        a center of gravity
        a thermal spring
        a magnetic field
        a mercurial planet

Survey
        Savor
this succulent atlas

Cherish
        Touch
               Connect

QUENCH

Quench me Quench
I parch with desire
Thirst is my fate
thirst is my fire

I bet with my tongue
I pant with my need
for the juicy joy
of liquid seed

Drown my desert
Deliver me drench
I crave the delectable
death of quench

I desire   I thirst for
the wet of fire

SONG OF THE GODBODY

I breathe you   I contain you   I propel you
I am your opening and closing
I am your rising and falling
I am your thrust and surrender

I stiffen you   I melt you   I energize
I quicken your humor and heartache
I set the spark to your fluid
I stir your mixable blessing

I am your inside operator
I stretch   I sweat   I maneuver
I flex your will and your man power
I polish your launching pad

I prime your engines of quest
I fan your spontaneous combustion
I drive your vehicles of dreams
I accelerate your valor and risk

I am at the root of your folly
I am at the top of your form
In you I caper and flourish
In you I become what I am

You are my cheerful vicissitude
You are my sturdy weakness
I am your faithful bedfellow
I am your tenacious secret

I connect your links
I replenish your seeds
I bathe in your bloodstream
I bask in the raw of your nature

I am the conductor of pulse and impulse
I am the director of anatomical play
You are my theater of nervous charades
You are my circus of knack and bungle

I am your unheeded prompter
I am the slips of your tongue
I am the catch in whatever you think
I am the quirk in what you are sure of

I carry a lantern through your labyrinth
I call to you from your vitals
You hear me best when you marvel
You hear me least when you whimper
You are my ancient   You are my child
You are the brother of all your heroes
My earnest monkey   My ticklish lion
You are my zoo and my sanctum
I tune up your instruments
I play on your organs
I strum in your breast
I croon in your head

I elixirate your phallus
I enter your every orifice
I impregnate every beginning
I effervesce   I rhapsodize

You plunge into motley waters
You catch me on fire when you love
You are my liquid opal
You are my burning bush

I sprout your sperm and your egg
I spawn the engodments of flesh
I shape the new body of Adam
I reshape the old body of Eve

I engender all the women of men
I generate the men of all women
I love you in every man's body
I live you in every man's lover

Trust that I know my own business
Cherish your fact and your fettle
Respect your perpetual motion
Relish your frisky divinity

You are my ripening godling
You are my fidgety angel
You are my immortal shenanigan
You are my eroding monument

I am ever your lifelong bodyguard
I am always your marathon dancer
Let your feet itch with my glory
Dance all the way to your death

DANCE OF THE GODBODY

I saw the Rhythm of the World rise out of the sea
I saw the waves roll back   the sands overturn
the breathing of the tides become a swimmer dancing
I saw the Godbody come ashore at the western sea

I had gone to the ocean in despair of the earth
despairing of the men who rule   and set the rules
men afraid to trust   afraid to caress
but quick to abuse   condemn   and slaughter

Then I saw the Swimming Dancer hurdle up the beach
rippling the world in the wind of his motion
The cliff   the tree   the cloud   the mountain
everything pulsed with the flow of his running

As I ran to catch up with him
I bumped headon into a giggling multitude
clods   drones   stumbling generations
all humanity fidgeting blindly in his train

On your toes! he cried   Keep in step with the cosmos!
You are all performers in the ballet of everything
and I am your choreographer for whatever move
    happens
I am everyone's dancing master till the end of tempo!

When he had vanished into the weather of the world
I knew then and forever how hubbubs can harmonize
At the edge of the world I met the Invisible Maestro
and the music of his dance keeps the singing in my days

GOD IS MY BELOVED

God is my Beloved
God and I are lovers
He lifts me in tidal embraces
         that turn the world on end

God is my Beloved
the ultimate in lovers
We ride through timeless spaces
         a rapture without end

God is my Beloved
from first to last my lover
I surrender to him in praises
         and never ask the end

THIS WONDER
A Hymn to Herm
(Duet for Tenor and Baritone)

This wonder
this prize
this secret
this wonder
my wonder
my steering gear
my sword
my bird in hand

this wonder
this surprise
this skyrocket
your wonder
our wonder
my takeoff
my songbird
my flying carpet

Your wonder
your catalyst
your talisman
your whirligig
your power dive
your up and about
your zingy dingbat

O wonder
your alchemist
your telescope
your wishbone
your parachute
your wanting-out
my fiddly twiddlestick

That wonder
that sidewinder
my chariot
my harlequin
my parsnip
my spark plug

that wonderer
that spellbinder
your chimney
your hyacinth
your percolator
your pressure cooker

This wonder
this pitchfork
this bagpipe
this homerun
this noble savage
this strip-squeeze
this twingey ginger jangle

this wonderful
this plumb line
this trombone
this touchdown
this undercover agent
this if-you-please
this rammycackle juggler

Your shillelagh
your yardstick
your cucumber
your skewer
your bullet
your voodoodle diddledad

my ukulele
my niblick
my can opener
my screw driver
my blowtorch
my abracadabra rattlesnake

This wonder
this tingle twick
this digit itch
this thistle paw
this lollipopper
this hornswoggler
this sizzly whang-dilly

this wonder kit
this tickle nip
this fingerswitch
this wiggle claw
this piledriver
this cornucopia
this whizbang whistle bag

This wonder
this jackknife
this rocket pad
this nose cone
this bombsight
this boing boing boomerang

this wonderwork
this jump-start
this meteor
this comet tail
this boomstick
this dingdong bongo bongo

Your one-up
your presto log
your bayonet
your tremolo
your pollywog
your holy cow

your one-hell-of-a
your flame-thrower
your barometer
your arpeggio
your pachyderm
your hallelujah

This wonder
this wonder
this pygmy
this salamander
this ground swell
this typhoon
this four-in-hand firing squad
this tightrope boiling point

to wonder at
to wander with
this Beowulf
this Hercules
this earthquake
this tidal wave
this five-finger spacewalk
this grand slam battering ram

this nozzle-blister
  nuzzle-switcher
this humdingery
  mainspringer
this rub-a-double
  bubble-burster
this out-of-hand
  walloping whopped

this hickery dickery
  dockablock
this sphincterrific
  sockdollager
this whim-whammy
  cream whipper
this out-of-sight
  sleight-of-hand
  killer-diller

Your wonder
from wonder
unfolding
all forms
all mine
all ways
this wonder
this wonder
this wondert
O!

and my wonder
into wonder
exploding
all formations
all ours
all the way
this wonder
this wonder
his wonder
O!

OLD SCORPIO

Poems of Old Age

75 LIFE LINES (1988)

Everything is perfect as it is
except for the things that haven't yet got it right.

*

Nothing is new. Everything is renewal.
Life's major challenge: getting reborn often enough.

*

Since we are formed of cosmological dust
let's clasp one another and kick up a storm.
Only to the enraptured does the prophetic speak.

*

If you feel completely at a loss
you are probably on the right track.

*

Since nobody knows the meaning of existence,
the limits of the universe, or the cure for a cold,
we are free to delight in the mysteries of ignorance.

*

Innocence is the holiness of sagacity.

*

Believe the unbelievable. Enliven the unlikely.
Always carry change for the unchangeable.

*

What distinguishes one human from another:
the capacity to love and the ability to wonder.

*

Wonder is my pleasure, love is my elation,
friendship is my hobby, rapture my vocation.

*

People live in their wrongheads,
not in their right minds.

*

Most minds oscillate between sense and nonsense.
The rest don't oscillate at all.

*

People who take a dim view of life
dwell in a murky doldrums.
The easiest thing to find is fault.

*

Many nobodies who have studied nothing
are busy teaching it to everybody else.

*

Everyone needs a hole in the head
to let out the pollution.
The lowest common denominator sinks lower every
day.

*

A dull prospect befogs the road to derring-do.
Exchange your mind for one with a better view.

*

Men are windowless monads
waiting for someone to raise their blinds.

*

People don't grow up. They just get taller.
People don't change. They just get more so.
Adults are deteriorated babies.

*

I love all men, except for those I can't stand.

*

When there's nothing you can do about anything,
do everything you can.

*

Muster the agile and compassionate.
Educate a humanity that will not embarrass the earth.

*

Stand firmly, sit serenely,
mutter profoundly, sing recklessly,
dance all the way to your death.

*

You are capable of extraordinary actions:
you can pee, sneeze, fart, puke, snore, shiver.
Are you sufficiently amazed by your mechanisms?

*

Your soul goes out to the ends of your toes.
Go with it!
It walks around everywhere on two legs.

*

We contain as much as we can imagine.
When we dance we jiggle the stars.

*

Make your home in left field. There's more room there.
Everybody wants to be in the right.

*

Never disown your mad superstitions,
bad habits, unclad fantasies,
Those are the riches of your personality.

*

Three cheers for agony, muddle and euphoria.
Without them there would be nothing to read.

*

The greatest enemies of the public good
are education, religion and the law.
What's good for the public it never gets:
riotous living and peace of mind.

*

The heavyhanded and the leadfooted
keep crowding one off the dance floor.

*

Dreary food is the main cause of social unrest.
Winedrinkers know the merriment of the blessed.

*

Governments are a conspiracy of the mad and the
inane.
Pass laws for the abolition of laws!

*

Don't fall asleep at the wheel of fortune.
Don't exercise, dance. Don't diet, chuckle.
Don't tell people what not to do.

*

Crazy old men are essential to society.
Otherwise young men have no suitable models.

*

Be fond, not wary.
Fear of love is fear of the sublime.

*

Every penis is on the firing squad of creation.
Every penis wants to belong to a new Adam.

*

Never resist any temptation. Except celibacy.

*

Be generous with joy and juicy with ripening.
Amplitude is the shape of splendor.

*

Enrich your repetoire of useless acts.
Watch waterfalls, sniff lilacs,
reply to meadowlarks, attack artichokes

*

It is harder to love the world than to denounce it,
harder to embrace existence than to renounce it.

*

Reality isn't made of concrete. It's a seminal soup.
Savor it, swim in it, season it with piss and vinegar.

*

Your instincts are mythical heroes
eager to launch impossible adventures.

*

Do not die without learning what you can
accomplish.
Fervor is eager to explode in all your molecules.

*

Misery is not an ultimate truth.
Authentic wisdom is a laughing matter.

*

Happiness takes a risk, misery plays it safe.

*

Wisdom is the least popular goal of humanity.
To be wise one must be foolish, foolhardy and
foolproof.

*

Overthrow the tyranny of the humorless.
Commit the dead serious to funeral homes.
Trust only what opens, what reveals, what lights up.

*

Everything that is, is Light.
Except on very dark days.

*

Make florid mistakes. Laugh more and wash less.
Eat more chocolate than beans. Fuck often.

*

Desires are not bushes to be pruned.
A man is not meant to be a bonsai.

*

Life's essentials:
champagne, furry slippers, foreplay.

*

Buddha was a nil-boy killjoy
Life is not a suffering duty.
Desire awakes the sleeps of beauty.

*

Cultivate your own form of workaday lunacy.
Otherwise you can't feel at home in the world.

*

If you soften your brain, it won't get brittle.
Add nuts when you go bananas.

*

When you have to fight fire with fire,
go jump in the lake.

*

Open your jocular vein! Spurt jocosity!
Laughter like garlic is a flavorsome cure-all.

*

Offend the righteous: ramble, dawdle, dabble.
And picnic in the cemetery.

*

Introduce your heart to the practice of hilarity
or the Good Life will prove a lifelong rarity.

*

Sexual orgies are less harmful to society
than political parties.

*

More and more profligacy!
How else shall we all connect?
One good fuck is worth a hundred debates.

*

Sexuality is the sport of the gods.
Eternity is in love with orgasm.

*

We fall in love in order to experience
bodily upheaval and spermatic visions.
This causes us to shudder and sweat,
exude gummy verbiage and sprout wings.

*

Love should unite mankind,
not split it up into exclusive couples.

*

Two things for lovers are a must:
equality of soul and mutual lust.

*

Hook up some chariots of chum.
We are already late for the camerado races.

*

Leave pigeonholes to pigeon droppings.

*

Change everything, except what you love.
Love everything that changes your mind.

*

To keep from feeling degraded by the times
bathe in a brook, sleep in a barnyard,
hula in the office, somersault in church.

*

Come live with me and be my life
and we shall have no need of wife.

*

Reaching what you can is not enough.
Reach what you cannot!

*

Strengthen lofty connections.
Muses and angels want to be called on,
gods appreciate a pat on the back.

*

God is man's largest diversion.
And man is God's favorite toy.

*

Recipe for the creative life: remove safety belts,
plug loopholes, burn down safe retreats,
get reborn often, compose like a frolicsome child,
and never ask the end.
*Serve forth your ripeness before it rots.

*

Live   Love   Laugh   Leap
Sing   Swim   Sink   Sleep

THINKING ABOUT DEATH

How often do you think about Death?
Death thinks about you all the time
Death is fatally in love with you and me
and his lust is known to be relentless

Life is an equally persistent lover
He was desiring each of us before we were born
I try to remain faithful to him   but I know
the relationship can't go on forever

Life relishes my body heat   my heartbeating
my blood   my semen   even my steamy notions
Death cherishes what is cool and mysterious in me
all that is shadowy and perverse like him

I like to think of Death awaiting our rendezvous
in a candlelit corner of an intimate café
where he will regale me with scandalous tales
of misbehavior in other worlds

Yet in the end it is Life that wears us out
At that crosswalk what will the traffic bear?
Shouldn't we think about Death more often?
Death is thinking about us all the time

WHEELCHAIR IN THE FAR WEST

When I hoarded blueprints for a jocund city
where the rights of the daft would be civil law
I combed the atlas for magnanimous harbors

Now on the shipwreck end of adventure
when my daily order reads Stay Awake!
my timbers are too shivered for a maiden voyage

Expeditions to colonize an Elysian Isle
must await launching in some other lifetime
Today my horizon has shrunk to a bathtub

Creeping decrepitude, crawl away!

WAITING FOR A LIFT

Though always I hoped to collapse upward
maybe a cozy miraculous uplift
is not guaranteed by the divine arms
Is surrender only allowed downward?
Must one hibernate in the dark earth
to wait for some elevating wake up call?

It is rumored that Jesus is in the neighborhood
looking for some body to resurrect

DEFECTIVE WIRING

I labored to embrace light
in as many encounters
as I could turn on.

Have you ever tried to
take the world in your arms?
It resists being fondled.

Out all day setting fires
under crotches
that refuse to burn.

Now that it's dark I
stay close to my hearth
and leave the porchlight on.

I want Death to feel welcome,
I look forward to
dazzling dawns at his house.

OLD SCORPIO ON OAHU

Don't worry about it.
if you are melting
that's the way it goes.
Especially if you are
an ice water sign.

I love to wade
the warm sea
love to feel my feet
turn fluid
If I dissolve neatly
what more is there to ask?

No longer at any
tiptop tiptoe
I can still
relish the extra
in the ordinary,
can still take hold
of the fire
with my watery hands.

THE BEACHED CRUISER

I am
a moony old vessel,
I have
garbled many a hanker.

Now I sit
by the ocean of notions.
I sit
on the dry land of facts.

Although
the winds still blow fevers
I know
what my timbers are made of
And now that I've got things cleared up
I can cheerfully rot in the sun.

BIG JOY, OCTOGENARIAN

An Interview With James Broughton

BIG JOY, OCTOGENARIAN:
AN INTERVIEW WITH JAMES BROUGHTON

James Broughton, dubbed "Big Joy" by Jonathan Williams, died peacefully at home on Monday, May 17, 1999, bringing to an end a long and extremely varied career. I interviewed James a number of times on my radio show. This last interview took place in Broughton's home in Port Townsend, Washington on November 9, 1997, the day before his eighty-fourth birthday. Its subject was his then new book, *Packing Up for Paradise: Selected Poems 1946-1996*. Selections from the interview were broadcast on my radio show on April 1 and April 8, 1998. What follows is the complete interview.

> I pray every night to wake up crazier
> If my balmy days last I may end as I began
> a dreamysmile Buddhafaced son of a gunman
> from way out west where the sunny boys come from
> — James Broughton, "Resume"
> (1982)

JACK FOLEY: One of the pleasures of having this job is that occasionally you can interview somebody who's a really wonderful poet and whose work you've admired for many, many years, as I've admired James Broughton's. We're in Port Townsend, where James lives, and James is about to turn 84 years "young," as they say. He's looking at me. I'm not so sure he likes that "young." Most people in their eighties are lucky if they are still able to function, let alone produce poems. James has been producing wonderful poems of his old age. Why don't we begin with the opening poem of the new book, *Packing Up for Paradise*.

JAMES BROUGHTON:

OPEN TO QUESTION

In a cool neck of the woods
a long walk from the village
I hide out from grunge and glitz
and pray for a tidy apocalypse.
Nothing much on my mind but
Love, God and Hereafter.

Though time is closing down
my life is still open to
whatever comes next
or whatever comes last.
With a shortening longevity
I need to consider last resorts.

A houseboat on the Styx
A villa in Elysium?
A bedroll in the Void?
Where is my inevitable home?
Is that the ultimate surprise?
(1996)

JACK FOLEY: Is it the "ultimate surprise"? We'll see. "Open to Question," with all that phrase might mean, you've often self-published beautiful editions of your books. For your birthday you made a little chapbook, eighty-four copies, one for each of your years, and Joel Singer made a beautiful image for the cover. It's of a baby James moving quickly through the cosmos as if he were a water baby. The chapbook is called *Big Joy* (Syzygy Press, 1997). Why not read the opening poem, which is in "E Major," as you mention.

JAMES BROUGHTON:

HYMN TO BIG JOY
In E Major

He He Oh He
He is the completest jolly of a He
He is the immaculated jeu d'esprit
He is the aorta's jigamaree

He Oh He He
His is the reekingest smell of free
His is the deafening fart of glee
His is jocosity's apogee

Oh He He He
laughiest daffiest verity

JACK FOLEY: You're quite serious in talking about that as "E Major." That sound of "e" goes all the way through that poem. Tell us a little bit about "the tone leading of vowels" as part of your procedure as a poet.

JAMES BROUGHTON: I can't write a line without feeling the music of it or the music that grows out of it. By now in my life, after 84 years, [it's] the automatic play of vowels and consonants. I learned long ago ... from Olson was it? "the tone leading of vowels" [the phrase is from Robert Duncan, ed.] and how they hit the consonants. It doesn't mean you always have the same vowel emphasized throughout the poem, as in this one. But you're aware of what's happening. Those sounds are the ones which echo.

JACK FOLEY: "Hymn to Big Joy" is a delightful little poem, reminiscent of William Blake's "Laughing Son." Your "Hymn" is full of e's, and so that "E Major" is very important, but the "He He Oh He"—that's laughter ("hee hee") but it's also "he," a person, and the person ("hymn," "him") is in fact "Big Joy," "the completest jolly of a he." There's a lot that's going on here. We hear the sound of "Big Joy," which is this he/e sound, all the way through the poem: "verity," "apogee," "glee," "free," "reeking," etc. Once you hear that "e"—once you hear that sound of joy—it echoes throughout.

JAMES BROUGHTON: Yes. It's like hearing a certain sound—a percussion sound—in a piece of music. Every time the player hits a delightful note, you refer to that, you bounce along on it. Like a xylophone. But Big Joy to me is also a serious matter too.

JACK FOLEY: Yes. In E Major.

JAMES BROUGHTON: People always say to me: "What do you mean by 'Big Joy'?" "Who is Big Joy?" What a dumb question!

JACK FOLEY: Absolutely. It's very clear who Big Joy is.

JAMES BROUGHTON: Joy is the secret of the universe. It comes from love, which rules the universe. And Big Joy is what runs the whole machine.

JACK FOLEY: It's a turn-around, too. J, B: James Broughton. B, J: Big Joy.

JAMES BROUGHTON: Jonathan Williams named me Big Joy.

JACK FOLEY: With good reason. In a century that has been full of murder, pollution, every other terrible thing, you have persistently written poetry about joy. You are the most positive poet of my acquaintance!

JAMES BROUGHTON: I can't help it! (Laughter) I'm often accused of being too cheerful. But that's just the way life is for me. I love to smile at adversity.

JACK FOLEY: One of the traditional things that poetry has been able to do is to help people in adversity. If you feel bad, you go to a poem and you feel comforted. And you give your reader that feeling.

JAMES BROUGHTON: I do that. I can tell from my fan mail that comes from strangers, all the time.

JACK FOLEY: That's a very odd thing for a "Modern" poet to be doing. It's a wonderful thing for a poet to be doing.

JAMES BROUGHTON: That's more important to me than "being a poet"— that is, functioning in the business of poetry. That career poetry has never interested me. But what it can do for other people, what it can say, what it can transform in their lives—to me, that's essential. Nothing is gained, nothing is lost, everything transforms.

JACK FOLEY: Like water.

JAMES BROUGHTON: And people are stuck in the past and in the future. But if you're right here now, you're transforming. That's a simple thing, but it seems to meet so much resistance.

Jack Foley: It does. It's a simple thing to say but it's a difficult thing to grasp fully. Your poetry has always been able to do that, to grasp it fully. You have written in more styles than any ten or twelve people one knows. The poetry is an embodiment of transformation. Harder to hit a moving target!

JAMES BROUGHTON: If I believe in anything, it's that: transformation.

JACK FOLEY: That includes the "transformation" of death. You have a section of the new book, *Packing Up for Paradise*, which is not called "Joie de Vivre" (Joy of Living) but "Joie de Mourire" (Joy of Dying).

JAMES BROUGHTON: Yes, yes. I'd like to read you a poem in which Big Joy is seen in a different light. This is called "What Big Joy Knows" (Big Joy):

> *I arise from the source of that sea*
> *formed by the tears of the world*
> *I swim with the dance of dolphins*
> *I float on the song of whales*

I hear what waves say to the shore
and what breezes sing to a leaf
I share the agonies of a beetle
and the anxieties of a planet

I know how to hurdle the road blocks
and what begins at the dead end
I keep the addresses of angels
and the unlisted number for God

JACK FOLEY: Again, water: "I arise from the source of that sea / formed by the tears of the world." That figure of the savior of one kind or another, always divine but always physical as well, has been in your poetry almost from the beginning.

JAMES BROUGHTON: Yes, saviors.

JACK FOLEY: A fire figure often, because you're a water sign, a Scorpio. That figure transforms too. It's so interesting to see it coming back in so many manifestations.

JAMES BROUGHTON: I remember a lyric I wrote several years ago, "What is Burning in the Deep?"

What is burning in the deep
far below the floating sail?
What is burning in the waters
down down within the whale?
What is burning in the deep
far below the rolling wave?
What is smoldering in the ashes
of Poseidon's blackened grave?

What is burning in the deep
from Atlantis's farewell?
What is flaming to be harrowed
from the ocean's salty hell?

What is burning in the deep
that churns the breakers with desire?
What new creature, what new city,
what new godhead is afire?

(1965)

JACK FOLEY: Yes! It was beautifully set and sung by the late Chilean singer, Ludar in his CD of your poems, The Broughton Songs. One of the things that will be very clear from Packing Up for Paradise is that there is recognition of suffering and of pain in your poetry at the same time that there is this wonderful thrust towards joy. But the thrust towards joy comes with the recognition of what pain is. How do we know what suffering is unless we suffer? This is represented in your poetry too. "Songs for Anxious Children" is one of your titles. You're wonderful on this. You never sentimentalize childhood. What you do instead is to present childhood with all its anxieties. You know about fears in childhood.

JAMES BROUGHTON: Well, suffering can't be avoided in life. Nobody ever said life was easy. The idea is to take it and, well, treat it like a football or something, bounce it in the air or make love to it. The only way you transform anything is by loving it.

JACK FOLEY: And by admitting that it's there, which is a problem for a lot of people.

JAMES BROUGHTON: You have to admit it's there, of course: acknowledge it.

JACK FOLEY: I remember one of the things you said in an interview on the World Wide Web. Many people say, "If I increase my consciousness, if I increase my self-awareness, I'm going to really mess up my poetry because I don't want to know what's happening." You say the opposite of that—that consciousness is a marvelous thing.

JAMES BROUGHTON: Absolutely. Because I think the way to happiness is to go into the darkness of yourself. That's the place the seed is nourished, takes its roots and grows up, and becomes ultimately the plant and the flower. You can only go upward by first going downward. I've never been afraid of losing my beautiful neurosis as a source of my poetry. (Laughter)

JACK FOLEY: Matthew Fox remarks that we've had enough "enlightenment." We now need some "endarkenment." In connection with that, I want to quote a little poem that's in that interview as well as in *Packing Up for Paradise*:

WHAT MATTERS

What matters
matters
but it doesn't

Some of the time
everything
matters

Much of the time
nothing
matters

In the long run
both everything
and nothing

matter a lot

(1993)

What matters matters, but it doesn't.

JAMES BROUGHTON: That's so important.

JACK FOLEY: (To the radio audience) I walked into James's house yesterday and he was just sitting there in the light. I've known James for a number of years and I've loved James for a number of years, as does everybody who knows him. James lights up a room! But as I walked in, I wasn't sure whether that light were going to be dimmed. I knew he had had a serious stroke and I knew he still had trouble walking and trouble writing—just the physical act of writing. I wasn't sure what I would find and I walked in, and there he was, radiating James! It was a wonderful moment for me, though when I mentioned it he waved his hand and said, "Well, you know this is just a masquerade." James, lots of painful things have happened to you recently. Yet one can feel the spirit still coming through. You are a living example of what you're talking about. You are "Joy" in the sense you talk about it: being able to transform adversity.

JAMES BROUGHTON: I think you have to let Joy grow inside you. You have to allow it. I don't believe in renunciations of any kind. I don't think that's the way to Enlightenment; I don't think that's the way to God. Not renunciation: acceptance, surrender, participation in everything in the glories of life. God is in everything. Embrace the fact that the mystery is everything we see and everything we don't see. And dance in that joy! Often my poems end by urging the reader to dance. Dance to your death, dance now.

JACK FOLEY: "Joie de Mourir." You say this about film as well. Some people think of film as being like painting. No, no, no, you say. It's not like painting. It's like dancing.

JAMES BROUGHTON: It is. I like to watch films like ballets—just watching them move. That's one of the great pleasures of cinema to me. Not what they're thinking or saying or their characterizations or the brilliant dialogue. I love the movement.

JACK FOLEY: Often in your films there will be moment in which everything is still. There's a moment in *Mother's Day* in which nothing is moving except that the breeze is moving a person's hair just a little bit. And you have "living statues" in your films as well. That goes back to your experience in vaudeville.

JAMES BROUGHTON: Vaudeville, and the circus as well. I think it was called

"The Sells-Floto Circus." A tent. In Modesto. My grandfather took me to the circus. Two rings, probably. Horses ran around and dogs and things. In the center there would be this velvet circular canopy. It would go up, and here would be these ladies in body stockings looking like they were nude, posed in Classical poses. "The Three Graces" and all that kind of thing. It would go up and they'd hold it, and then it would come down again and then they'd do another one. I thought that was amazing. I wasn't paying any attention to the clowns at that point. I was seeing Greek art—living, "living statues." Something about that: the beauty of the human body is the greatest statue there is, and it's a living statue. It moves and dances and sings and speaks brilliantly sometimes. But that's not the important thing. The beautiful thing is the body as the temple of the soul.

JACK FOLEY: And "body" has been an absolutely central interest of yours throughout your career.

JAMES BROUGHTON: Maybe that's why I'm still in my body at eighty-four!

JACK FOLEY: Someone suggested that it was your lover Joel Singer's cooking that kept you on the earth. The idea was that you certainly wouldn't want to "transform" yourself and miss that.

JAMES BROUGHTON: Yes. I think about my dear colleagues who are gone, like Duncan and Spicer and so on, and I remember how much vitriol they had in them, and I wonder whether that didn't hasten their early deaths.

JACK FOLEY: If you live long enough, you have reason for great bitterness. Everybody does. A lot of things go wrong in a life. That's simply not the case for you, one detects no bitterness—which is quite a wonderful thing.

JAMES BROUGHTON: Yes, you find out it doesn't matter.

JACK FOLEY: As you've said, you fed your bitterness some gumdrops.

JAMES BROUGHTON: Yes! You have to recognize the demons or else they'll annoy you like mosquitoes. But if you acknowledge their existence, if you say, "All right, here's a cookie, go sit in the corner," then you can go about your work and you don't have to go into deep depression because of it.

JACK FOLEY: Both your parents died young, so it must have been quite an amazement for you to be living—longer.

JAMES BROUGHTON: I should say so!

JACK FOLEY: *Packing Up for Paradise* is certainly a bit of candy for your bitterness. (To the radio audience) James, once, in a very un-James-like moment, mentioned some things which were going wrong; even James had been gotten down by these things, and he complained a little bit. I said, "Well, I know something you should read." He said, "What?" I said, "The works of James Broughton would be a wonderful antidote to the way you're feeling just now." (Returning to James) I don't know whether you went and read some of your own works.

JAMES BROUGHTON: (Laughing) You know what can cheer me up? This is not narcissistic, but it's a true thing. When I want to read something that will cheer me up, I re-read my memoir, *Coming Unbuttoned.* I think it's amazingly well-written, for prose. I wrote the prose as carefully as I write poetry. And it certainly works that way. The attitude towards life expressed in that book always cheers me up. I feel a little like that character in *The Importance of Being Earnest*—Gwendolyn, was it? She said, "I always take my journal on the trains so I'll have something interesting to read." I always take my memoir. It bears re-reading—even by the author! (Laughter)

JACK FOLEY: Especially by the author. And especially when the author is feeling a little low. It will bring you high again. It reminds you of your life.

JAMES BROUGHTON: Yes, of course.

Jack Foley: Part of it too is your description in that book of your wonderful encounter with your angel, your genius.

James Broughton: Yes, that reminds me, too. Then I think, "Where are you?" And I can call him. Things like that out of the book.

Jack Foley: Are you still in contact with the angel?

James Broughton: Oh, yes, of course! He's my familiar.

Jack Foley: I recently did an interview with James Hillman, and he sees such figures, angels, as very important. In his book *The Soul's Code,* he talks about the Dæmon, in the Neoplatonic sense—not demon but *dæmon.* This can be the Guardian Angel or any number of other things. Quite clearly, what you've done in your books is an expression of that angelic encounter. And you did it very early on.

James Broughton: I was encouraged in this very early on by a librarian, who was quite an interesting woman. She told me she had a little angel, which was for her like a little imp, who sat on her left shoulder and talked into her ear. I thought, "That's wonderful." Then I thought, "Oh, I have one, but he doesn't come that way."

Jack Foley: (referring to *Coming Unbuttoned*) He makes you "wet your jammies"!

James Broughton: Yes. He gives me wonderful shivers and tickles me. He knows where I giggle. Besides which, he's always just a few years older than I.

Jack Foley: At this point that's harder to do!

James Broughton: Oh, I know, but he's still beautiful, he still can fly around! This is interesting: At night, I sometimes feel him blowing on the back of my head. My hair goes—

And I think, "There's no wind in this bedroom, how weird!" And then I realize who it was.

JACK FOLEY: I just mentioned that scene in *Mother's Day* where only a person's hair is blowing. I didn't know the angel was doing it! Another thing that's so fascinating in your work—we're talking about almost fairy creatures: I was speaking to a friend of mine who lives in New Jersey, a writer who knows your work and loves it. We were saying that Broughton has never had much success on the East coast. Partly it was that you're from California, partly it was homophobia. But the friend of mine was gay and certainly there have been successful gay writers on the East coast. We realized that it wasn't just homophobia. It was that you were (to use a word that you use) deliberately and actively and in-your-face: "sissy."

JAMES BROUGHTON: Yes, I wanted to be a wonderful faery! They always tickled children, they danced among the flowers and sparkled. They embodied light. And that's why I always felt close to them.

JACK FOLEY: You told radio interviewer Robin White that, after the "final" transformation, you'd probably go zooming through the cosmos.

JAMES BROUGHTON: Oh, I don't know. Never ask the end, that's very much my approach to the Beyond.

JACK FOLEY: One of your mottoes is "Adventure, not Predicament."

JAMES BROUGHTON: I think the mystery shouldn't be explained. You can't explain it, it's a mistake.

JACK FOLEY: You've pointed out that you have been writing farewell poems for many years now. It's a mystery you have explored.

JAMES BROUGHTON: Oh, yes. Will the last gasp be the great breathtaking event? I'm always asking those questions, I guess. I look forward to it. But I have no fixed idea about it at all. I read these popular books about people who had near-death experiences and they saw this wonderful light and their whole lives went by. I don't want to know that. I want to have my own wonder going around the corner.

JACK FOLEY: Perhaps one of the ways of dividing people is to see them either as people who wish to know or people who wish to stay in a state of what Keats called "Negative Capability"—not to know and to allow the mystery to manifest; to lose themselves in the mystery.

JAMES BROUGHTON: I think people are absolutely wrong to want to know why. That's not the approach to the mysteries of the universe, "why." The approach is to celebrate them. Everything I've done has been a celebration.

JACK FOLEY: Your work is so distinctive, so different from anything else that's going around, the parallels one thinks of are really stretches. One might say you're like Cole Porter or Dorothy Parker. But you're not much like them. There's always something that goes beyond. There's always something in even the simplest Broughton poems that moves you a little beyond the poem, nudges you a little, pushes you in a direction which is no longer quite what that kind of poem was. Transforms you. There's a great line in Rilke's poem, "*Archaischer Torso Apollos*" ("Archaic Torso of Apollo"): "*Du mubt dein Leben andern*" ("You must change your life"). Even the simplest and lightest-hearted of your poems are telling us exactly that.

JAMES BROUGHTON: Well, that's my message. What I say in a poem is becoming more and more important to me. I don't write poems as objects, as a project. I'm only interested in how it can awaken or delight or transform. Therefore when I say I want it to be clear, I'm not trying to sound more profound than anybody else. I'm trying to get closer to the mystery and let the mystery be. That's an e again—beee.

JACK FOLEY: Why don't we hear a little bit more of the poetry. These are new poems by a man well into his eighties. It's wonderful to have these poems. One can scarcely find any examples of poets at such an age producing work. You came up with one good example, Thomas Hardy. But there aren't many. We need the testimony of old age. What does it mean to be "older"?

JAMES BROUGHTON: This is called "Vehicles." It's appropriate perhaps to what you say.

> Bleeding in the emergency room
> I remembered Grandmother
> stricken in the Buick
> as she watched us splash
> in the irrigation ditch.
>
> Then Grandfather's easy chair
> sat for a year un-sat-in
> after he was taxied home
> from the Rotary Club
> without his shoes on.
>
> When our widowed neighbor
> in the mobile home park
> could no longer play tennis
> he went to bed and fasted
> till the hearse came for him.
>
> After the curb tripped my toe
> and banged me to the pavement
> I woke to a mouth full of blood
> and the ambulance driver's bark:
> Are you drunk? Dying? On drugs?
>
> I had been on my way to a church
> to hear Mozart's Requiem.
> When they take me for a final ride
> can there be just alleluias
> and no questions asked?
>
> (1995)

JACK FOLEY: That's a wonderful poem. All the things the word "vehicles" can mean.

JAMES BROUGHTON: This is called "Testimonies."

JACK FOLEY: The word "testimony" is etymologically connected to "testes"!

JAMES BROUGHTON: Is it!

TESTIMONIES

Said the fortune teller from Reno,
If you hope for high-flying stakes
in the touch-and-go tossup of life
don't count on the sky's limit.
Instead of silver in a cloud
gamble on gold in the mud.

Said the astrophysicist from Boston,
The day your calcium and iron
collided in a cosmic bang
your stardust began to beget.
Now in your cortex the gods
play pingpong with your life.

Said the window-washer from Dallas,
For years I tried to clarify
the purpose of smudge and blur.
When a glass wall split apart
and sent me flying through it
my vision of life cleared up.

Said the neophyte from Boulder,
Your life if unredeemable
until you have sat in worship
at the feet of a holy master
had your ego burned to a crisp
and been zapped by mystic radiance.

Said the one-armed logger from Portland,
Most of the time of your life
as you chip away the days
you think it is all monotony.
Then at the severance payoff
you realize it has all been magic.

(1991)

JACK FOLEY: There's a tendency in your work towards Buddhism. But there's also a tendency away from it.

JAMES BROUGHTON:I have a tendency towards all religions. I mean, I love them all. But I don't take them all straight. I never believed any theology, really. It was always just a jumping off spot.

JACK FOLEY: Religion might be considered fossilized poetry. You can see the poetry in it, but you better not fossilize it, otherwise you'll be stuck. And stuck is one of the things you least want to be.

JAMES BROUGHTON: Well, I was raised an Anglican and I loved the ritual, the music, and the sound of the wonderful King James English. (They don't use it any more, alas.) But all these things about "Oh, you miserable sinner"—I just looked the other way or else I closed my ears. I hate the whole idea of sin. It seems to me the most absurd idea ever turned loose in the world. Who said we were born sinners? What a ridiculous notion! Have they ever looked at a babe? When my son was born, the nurse said, "He looks like a little Buddha." Sin, indeed!

JACK FOLEY: You have a marvelous film in which you recite your poem, "This Is It." It's your son just walking down the street in Mill Valley. It's marvelous to watch that body move, to watch him bouncing along with his red cowboy hat.

JAMES BROUGHTON: That's why I made the film. He had this wonderful sense of being astonished by the world.

JACK FOLEY: Long after you'd been writing in this way, people began to talk about "the inner child." You've had an "inner child" going for you for many years!

JAMES BROUGHTON: You must take care of your inner child all your life. That's the one to raise, never mind your own children. They'll have to find for themselves anyway. This is a recent poem, "Momento of an Amorist":

> When the young interviewer wanted to know
> how he occupied his time in retirement
> the ailing novelist sat up on his couch
> to enjoy a guffaw before he spoke.
>
> I haven't a retiring bone in my body.
> I still slip out to pay my respects
> to the beauties passing across the world.
> Bless all mothers of shapely offspring.
> I've never met a cock I didn't like.
>
> Oh, said the reporter, may I quote that?
>
> Say that I give compassionate attention
> to mankind's need for a taste of bliss.
> Don't you appreciate a friendly fondle?
> To expect some love in return? Oh no.
> I never look for a lover. I am one.
>
> But sir, isn't such behavior risky?
>
> Don't flinch, dear fellow. Learn to adore.
> Adoration is life's healthiest behavior.
> Wherever you go be a passionate lover
> of whatever happens or whoever it is.
> You'll grin all the way to your grave.

When he was later assigned the obituary
the journalist read in the suicide note:
I never learned to distinguish between
illusion and miracle. I didn't need to.
I trusted in love's confusing joy.

(1996)

Isn't that marvelous. "Learn to adore. / Adoration is life's healthiest behavior."

JACK FOLEY: There was a remark Ezra Pound made when Harry Crosby committed suicide. Pound called it "suicide as a vote of confidence in the cosmos."

JAMES BROUGHTON: Yes!

JACK FOLEY: One of the problems for someone my age—late fifties—trying to write poetry. So many people die. How do you stop writing elegies?

JAMES BROUGHTON: You can't. I just wish my friends godspeed. This was written for my dear friend James Leo Herlihy: "Elegy with Bird." This is the same point:

Under an October drizzle
and a flurry of windy leaves
I walked around the lagoon
where the sanitation plant hums
and transient flocks pause for a float
en route to faraway nestings.

I walked at a funeral pace
lamenting the loss of my godfellow:
the fond crony of luminous wit
who had shared each intricate wish
in my heart's quixotic history
and never missed a nuance.

Amid the debris of autumn
beneath the windy and wet
I took refuge on a rough stone
to help my sorrow subside.
it wanted to petrify into
a sepulcher of tears.

But a startle of wings slapped the air
as a heron sailed over my head
in easygoing takeoff and flight
that set its unwavering course
for the tideland of the farther shore.
I leapt up to wave it Godspeed.

(1996)

JACK FOLEY: "Packing up for Paradise"! That's a beautiful elegy for your friend.

JAMES BROUGHTON: Of course we miss people. You can indulge your grief. But if you care about them you want to wish them godspeed. Into the arms of God.

JACK FOLEY: There's a beautiful image on the cover of *Packing up for Paradise*. It was done by Joel Singer. There's a golden train and there's a bird. Birds are of course so often associated with souls, as they are in your "Elegy." This bird isn't going to fly, he's going to take the train!

JAMES BROUGHTON: I also have a poem called "The Partner."

Sundays he watches me eat breakfast.
More often he turns up at bedtime.
On the street when I least expect it
he puts his arm around my shoulder
and breathes down my neck. I think
death is getting too intimate.

He volunteers to be my trust officer,
suggests I liquidate my holdings
and deposit the remains in his account.
Am I ready to cash in my worldly goods?
Does my life investment in lyric song
amount to anything redeemable?

If I go along with being his partner
and we set up business in his hometown,
how does he plan to get me there?

(1995)

JACK FOLEY: So many of your poems are questions—very interesting questions.

JAMES BROUGHTON: Yes, of course. There are no final answers to anything.

JACK FOLEY: One of the things to know about questions is that they don't have to have answers. Just the fact of asking a question sometimes is an indication of spiritual growth.

JAMES BROUGHTON: Exactly. I agree with you.

MY TORTOISE

Once my totem was a unicorn.
Now at a decelerating age
I settle for a tortoise.

He shuns push and shove,
snubs sidetrack and pit-stop,
has no traffic with hellbent,
prefers one plod at a time.

His backside discourages backslap
and claw, stinger and tooth.

Says the motto on his tattoo:
"Perseverance furthers."

If I nod off in my dawdle
he can persist to the finish
and leave footprints in the sand.

(1995)

(Quoting Longfellow's "A Psalm of Life," with its once-famous quatrain, "Lives of great men all remind us / We can make our lives sublime, / And, departing, leave behind us / Footprints on the sands of time") "Lives of great men remind us…" I don't have to leave my footprints. We all leave footprints somewhere.

JACK FOLEY: You grew up in a tradition of poetry, which was very different from "Modernism."

JAMES BROUGHTON: Yes, my grandmother's house was full of volumes of poems.

JACK FOLEY: You mentioned *The Rubaiyat of Omar Khayyam* to me earlier. Dangerous poetry for a little boy to be reading!

JAMES BROUGHTON: Tennyson, Longfellow. Whittier. And Elbert Hubbard, the author of *A Message to Garcia*. That's where I got my fascination of homely homilies. He was a very popular cheer-up man of his age. (Like Broughton's "My Tortoise," Hubbard's *A Message to Garcia* extols the virtue of perseverance—ed.)

Jack Foley: You harken back to a mode of poetry and a mode of understanding poetry that is not something that is current at all. People like Dana Gioia would like to get some of that back.

JAMES BROUGHTON: It's so strange when you read a poem of Byron's or Wordsworth's—they were so popular. They sold hundreds of thousands of copies right away. The appetite for good writing and for vocabulary (to say nothing of "the tone leading of vowels") is a dying art.

JACK FOLEY: When Ken Burns did a very nice series on the Civil War, people heard letters being read aloud and they said, "Isn't it wonderful, the 19th century had such a marvelous sense of literature." "Eloquence" was the word people used. But the funny thing was that the people were saying that because they were watching a TV show. It wasn't that they had read a book. It took the TV program to remind them of the virtues of literature!

JAMES BROUGHTON: If you read the newspapers of the middle of the 19th century, they're extremely literate. They have a marvelous sense of adverbs. And they know where the verb should be. Clinton can't speak like Lincoln. "Fourscore and seven years ago..."

JACK FOLEY: And Lincoln wrote it himself. Clinton isn't even able to speak like Kennedy, who didn't write his speeches himself. But at least Kennedy's speeches were fairly literate.

JAMES BROUGHTON: Literacy is a dying art. Isn't that sad.

JACK FOLEY: Distinctions that are part of language have begun to fall apart.

JAMES BROUGHTON: That's what I meant. My friend James Leo Herlihy could understand every nuance, every reference—how delightful, that's such a great joy. I used to be sad that my students would miss my most subtle, beautiful phrasing in a lecture. I'd wait. They'd still be chewing or asleep.

JACK FOLEY: Part of the joy of your work is the joy of reading somebody who loves to write and who loves words. You gave me a gift once of a book of rare words. You have great delight in words, great delight in thinking about words and where they might go. It's the source, really, of your literature. It's the source of your self. You mentioned adverbs a moment ago.

JAMES BROUGHTON: Yes. When you add them to a verb you get a subtle kind of movement the simple verb doesn't have. It's quite different from an adjective, which decorates, gives you a different feeling. This is a nuance in the texture that I like. When I started to write prose, I always found it very difficult because I always really thought in poetry. I like the succinct, the terse. I had to get around the fact that most sentences are just journalistic reports on an event, even in novels. I had to learn how to play with the sentence and really enjoy the sounds. To take a sentence in your hand and rock the words around until you've heard the sounds in the verbs and the consonants, so it was pleasing to the ear. It was Ezra Pound who said, "Poetry must be as well written as prose" (*The Letters of Ezra Pound 1907-1941*, #60, Harcourt, Brace, 1950). Most people who use prose don't know how to write it. "Is that what I've been speaking all my life?" as the man said in Moliere's play (*Le Bourgeois Gentilhomme*). They're so unconscious of the language. You have to have an ear and to enjoy speaking. But practice! It's like playing any instrument.

I just thought of something. The title, *Packing Up for Paradise*. It was the choice of my editor Jim Cory because he liked the poem, which is in this book. It isn't talking about what I expect after death. I don't intend to behave in my old ways. I'll be transformed. I'll be more graceful, more faery-like, more ebullient. Most of the time I'll just sit around in my universal mind.

I'll just read the last page of Big Joy:

P.S. FROM BIG JOY

Brillo your soul. Windex your spirit.
Here comes lucidity.

*

A blithe spirit brings a lark
into any bored room.

*

Relish everything
and keep nothing.
Pack up everything
but take it to the dump.

*

Never let go of abandon.
Applaud every flabbergast.

*

The worst is still to come
and the best is yet to be.

JACK FOLEY: That's another "e" sound. The book begins and ends with it. In between is a ride through consciousness.

JAMES BROUGHTON: The soul is consciousness. What we hope for or what this idea of Enlightenment means is consciousness in bliss, consciousness in bliss. That would be my recipe.

JACK FOLEY: For many, those two things, consciousness and bliss, would be opposites. Not for James.

JAMES BROUGHTON: No!

JACK FOLEY: Thank you, James.

BEHOLD THE BRIDEGROOMS

A connubial masque for James and Joel

BEHOLD THE BRIDEGROOMS
A connubial masque for James and Joel

Perhaps the best introduction to Broughton's not-merely-alchemical wedding celebration, "Behold the Bridegrooms," are these verses by the seventeenth-century poet Daniel Stolcius. They are from his alchemical work, *The Pleasure Garden of Chemistry* (1634) and are very much in the spirit of James Broughton:

> Destruction brings about
> Death of the material;
>> But the spirit renews,
>> Like before, the life.

> Hence the black globe
> Signifies the black raven.
>> Also the light spirit
>> Quickly expels human consciousness;

> Provided that the see is
> Putrefied in the right soil;
>> Otherwise all labor, work, and art
>> Will be in vain.

BEHOLD THE BRIDEGROOMS
A connubial masque for James and Joel

Participants

    THE GOD HERMEROS
    THE PRIEST
    THE BRIDEGROOMS
    THE FIVE POETS
    THE TWO ACOLYTES
    THE WEDDING GUESTS
    THE MUSICIANS

> *The Wedding Guests await in festive dress.*
> *The two Acolytes come out to them*
> *and distribute lighted tapers.*
> *Acolyte One wears a seablue gown,*
> *Acolyte Two wears a gown of flame-red.*

> *A joyful noise: bells and gamelan.*
> *Hermeros, spirit of the occasion, appears*
> *wearing mainly talaria and a chiton.*

HERMEROS

Dear friends of love, divest yourselves of grouch,
be intimate with cheer, be generous with caress.
For here at twilight on this venerable barge
an uncommon wedding shall be gaily solemnized.

I come to bid you welcome and to set the scene
for I am patron of such androgyne events,
being the special deity of inseparable men.
Hermeros am I called, since I was originated
by phallic Hermes in amorous sport with Eros.

Psyche and Hermaphroditus are my next of kin
so I defend impieties of the passionate
as well as improprieties of the ambivalent.
I guard the erogenous, the wise, the pulchritudinous,
And being particular friend to poets and visionaries
I come hence to put a Greekish blessing on this match.

Some cynic ones make jest of any marriage vows.
They scoff to see love's hot abandonments
tied up in bonded knots of mutual pledge.
Yet fervent oath and sacrament forever reaffirm
man's hearty lust for paradise on earth:
willingly would he enslave his life to ecstasy.

A long-destined choice of wedding will we here unfold
for these two souls have many times been betrothed,
in former lives were denied their love's desire.
Thus has their union waited centuries for this day
when we may cheer eternity's change of heart.

The music rings the bells! Espousal rites begin!
Move forward, fellow poets, bosom friends,
to take your places for this sanctifying joy.
Follow in procession the tintinnabulating sound,
carry your tapers brightly to the altar side
and find your witnessing standpoints in the hall.

The sacral lamps are lit, the frankincense and myrrh,
the pathway of fresh petals strewn across the deck!
The gong sounds the approach! Their coming we
    illuminate!
Behold the bridegrooms now! And jubilate!

> *Hermeros vanishes. The processional begins.*

> *The Priest enters, preceded by the censing Acolytes.
> The robed Poets take their places with the Guests.
> Last comes the Bridegrooms in gowns and
> garlands.*

PRIEST

Dearly beloved all,
be all loved dearly here!
Love is the free play of the Divine
and we are here to bring the Divine
freely into play.

These two who stand before me
have assembled us upon this floating temple
to share in their celebration of
the deep astonishments of divine grace.
They ask to be joined sacramentally to
the enravishments of their love.

Let us praise their fine audacity.
Let us praise their risk of happiness.
Let us raise our burning lights to them
to enlighten their burning hearts!

The Guests lift their tapers high.

Let us raise our lights even higher yet
to salute the ingenuities of the gods
who prepare our profound encounters
and conduct us to our fates.

With lights thus lifted let us chant thrice
the Pleasure Mantra of the World:
Aaahhh! Aaahhh! Aaahhh!

GUESTS

Aaahhh! Aaahhh! Aaahhh!

PRIEST

Now we may lower our separate flames
and make of them one single powerful light.
Come forward, each of you in turn,
to place your candle upright in the sacred cauldron
standing at mid-center of this hall.

Let each of our lights blaze together
One unified faith in the lights of love!

> *The Guests dispose their tapers in the*
> *sand-filled bowl.*

Now the first Poet will step forth to read
the Epithalamium for this wedding day.

FIRST POET

Ripe in the sunfall before the moonrise
here are we gathered here surrounded
upon the decks of art and philosophy
upon the waters and between the winds
Here are we gathered to surround two lovers
here are we witnesses to a grace of souls

Hale in the twilight before the moontime
above the fishes and beneath the birds
here are we surrounded by our faithful Guardians

gathered by our Angels of Recognition
Here are we partners to a boldness of hearts
here we gather love to surround these lovers

PRIEST

Beneath opposing forces were these souls born:
theirs is a conjunction of flame and wave,
of ember and ice, of furnace and fountain.

On this day, at the onset of Leo's yearly fire
with the moon aswim in the sea of Pisces,
we shall consummate here in significant union,
we shall unite Scorpio and Sagittarius
in a sprightly marriage of Fire and Water.

These powers who straddle the zodiac side by side
shall romp across its ecliptic in surprising harmony:

the Scorpion shall ride the Centaur through
the burning lake in the Milky Way.
Kneel now, bridegrooms both,
kneel to receive the alchemical blessing.

> *Solemn music. The bridegrooms kneel.*
> *Acolyte One brings from the altar*
> *one red and one blue candle.*
> *He holds the flames over the heads*
> *of the Bridegrooms.*

> *Acolyte Two brings a ritual vessel*
> *containing water from a Mt. Tamalpais*
> *spring and from the Pacific Ocean*
> *at Stinson Beach.*

> *With feathers from a pure white dove*
> *she sprinkles each Bridegroom three*
> *times, while tallow drips on them*
> *from the candles.*

This union triumphs in alchemical mystery.
This union transpires under the benediction
of the Divine Androgyne of All Things.
Let us hear then the Poet's Hymn to the
    Androgyne.

SECOND POET

Praise to the Androgyne   the All in One
Praise to his unbelievable truth
He loves us as we originally were
He loves us as we always are
    He is beyond the explicit
    He is the total union
    He is the transcendent single
    He is the doubles champion
He is woman man   he is goddess god
He is the seeder and the seeded

He is the Both   He is the And
He is the source and the sorcerer
            He is the her in the he
            He is the him in the she
            He is the two in the one
            He is the one beyond two
Praise to Androgyne   the Irreducible All
Praise to his unbelievable truth
He loves us as we originally were
Her loves us as we always are

PRIEST

These holy mysteries elucidate
The great enigmas of mankind.
We all are incarnations of the Androgyne.
We are mirror of the Godbody.

Dearly betrothed, look now upon each other
as you repeat in unison after me
the zealous paradoxes of your love:
You are my Lover   You are my Beloved

BRIDEGROOMS

You are my Lover   You are my Beloved

PRIESTS

You are my Parent   You are my Child

BRIDEGROOMS

You are my Parent   You are my Child

PRIEST

You are my Fate   You are my Soulmate

BRIDEGROOMS

You are my Fate   You are my Soulmate

PRIEST

You are my bridegroom   You are my Bride

BRIDEGROOMS

You are my bridegroom   You are my Bride

PRIEST

Now shall this company cheer these vows
by chanting the Pleasure Mantra three times.

GUESTS

Aaahhh!   Aaahhh!   Aaahhh!

PRIEST

Bring forth the grail with the communioning
liberation!
Bring it to the third Poet for his consecrating!

*Acolyte One brings forward
the ceremonial cup.*

THIRD POET

This cup contains an unearthly nectar
habitually served at the wedding of wizards.
It is compounded by local seraphs and satyrs
from apricotroot   appleheart   and plumtail
poppybrine   cashewegg   and salmonbreast
larksweat   lionspray   and mothsperm
distilled in the pearly honesty of the moon.
It contains the essence of spirits in delight:
the delicious secret of the Great Intoxication.
Everyone may risk one sip. Serve it forth!

*Acolyte One proffers the grail
first to each of the Bridegrooms.*

Then he brings it to each Guest in turn
and finally back to the Priest.

All during this communion the Third Poet
recites the Nectar Sutra repeatedly
until the communion concludes.

THIRD POET

Drink in remembrance of
  Adam   the Original Androgyne
  Hermes   the Passionate Shape-changer
  Krishna   the Love-spreading Flutist
  Jesus   the Bridegroom of the Godbody

Drink in remembrance of
  Shiva and his Shakti
  Rumi and his Shamsi
  Gilgamesh and his Enkidu
  David and his Jonathan

Drink in remembrance of
  Whitman and Plato
  Leonardo and Michelangelo
  Rimbaud and Cocteau
  Bach and Blake and the Bard of Avon

Drink in remembrance of all
  poets and charioteers
  philosophers and explorers
  siddhas and saints
  buddhas and bodhisattvas
And in salutation to
  all possible weddings of the gods
  on earth and in heaven

Acolyte Two brings the inlaid box
containing the wedding rings.

The Priest opens it and offers it in turn
to each of the Bridegrooms.

PRIEST

Here are the blinding circlets of gold
That proclaim your treasure to one another
and proclaim your devotion before the world.
Joel, as you place the ring of wedding
on your spouse's finger
speak whatever words ring in your heart.

JOEL

Jamie   my love

At your breast I taste our troth
my mother's milk through soulsweet sweat
Centuries of eyes I've looked for yours
Beloved bearded my white haired wizard
Chiseled years reveal your beauty

Let me carry you   Let me cry
my father's come the godspilled gift
a truth I treasure in my womb
O closer my Jamie   my child newborn
Let me wrap you   anoint you with peppery
          secrets

Let us be hawks   and the wind our bed
will carry the Yes on its breath
My Androgyne Bride   your secrets are safe
cherished within my temple

PRIEST

James, as you place the ring of wedding
On your spouse's finger
Speak whatever words ring in your heart.

JAMES

Beloved One   prize of my life
I proudly wed my soul to your flesh
You are the love I have longed for all my life
You are the love I thought I would never have
       in this life
You are the miracle that renews my life
My touchstone   my touchable angel
I am enfolded in your devotion
I am renewable in your rapture
You are my direct connection to the divine
You are my only and my rightful fate

I will drink love tonics from your mouth
I will absorb healing energy from your fingers
I will be nourished and renourished by your
       beauty
With you I will fill full   I will fulfill
I will abide till I disintegrate

PRIEST

These avowals deserve our happiest praise.
Let us repeat our Pleasure Mantra once again.

GUESTS

Aaahhh!   Aaahhh!   Aaahhh!

PRIEST

The Poet shall now read the Lesson for Today.

FOURTH POET

Here are the Now Commandments I give unto you.

Thou shalt   Thou shalt   And thou shalt
Thou shalt loosen   Thou shalt flow   Thou shalt flower
Thou shalt love   Thou shalt love   Thou shalt love

Thou shalt surrender the miseries of thy mind
Thou shalt retrieve the innocence of thy heart
Thou shalt relish the amazement of thy body
Thou shalt revel in thy dishevelment
Thou shalt commit ecstasies upon the earth
Thou shalt commit merriments to cheer the heavens
Thou shalt live   Thou shalt give   Thou shalt flourish
Thou shalt love   Thou shalt love   Thou shalt love
Thou shalt   Thou shalt   And thou shalt

PRIEST

Let the Lovers pledge their most intimate troth.
Let them come forth and proclaim their chakra vows.

> *The Bridegrooms stand in the center*
> *of the hall and bless with a kiss each*
> *chakra of the other, saying in turn:*

BRIDEGROOMS

I cherish you from
the bottom of your feet to
the crown of your head.

I honor the entire temple of your body
as a holy place of infinite joy.

I bless your centers of energy
your meridians of creation
your mandalas of bliss.

I kiss now the vital centers of your torso
from your perineum to your phallus
from your navel to your heart
from your throat to your third eye.

> *They embrace and are uplifted.*

PRIEST

In witness of these offerings of surrender
The blessing of bliss is upon all of us here.
Let us join in a Bliss Mantra.

FIFTH POET

Bliss   Bliss   Bliss
Bliss Us   Bliss Thus   Bliss This
Two Bliss   Both Bliss   Together Bliss
Vow Bliss   Now Bliss   Kiss Bliss
Body Bliss   Buddha Bliss   Beauty Bliss
Two-in-on Bliss   Two-in-wonder Bliss   Bliss
          Bliss
Bless Bliss   Bless Thus   Bless This
Bliss   Bliss   Bliss

GUESTS

Bliss!   Bliss!   Bliss!

PRIEST

Blissful Ones, be ever blessed.
Now I shall pronounce you
lovers for life   and livers for love
In all lifetimes and in all loveworlds.

BRIDEGROOMS

We thank you with our hearts and with our souls.
That you may wear our blessing as your own
we shall here encircle everyone with embrace
and with loverknots of commingled fire and water.

Fanfares. The Acolytes bring strands
of colored wool. The Bridegrooms
move among the Guests and tie
two threads, one flame-red and one
marine-blue, around every neck of the
assembled company. They also
bestow a kiss upon every check.
Hermeros reappears as an Epilogue.

HERMEROS

Our revels are not ended here, they only now begin.
Already champagne bottled blow their tops
to herald festive feasting for this night.
The largest tidbit shall be the wedding cake
with double bridegrooms in a sugared belvedere!

A wedding seems to promise delectable euphoria
while a marriage may produce vexation and dismay.
However, men like these whose love abounds in grace
possess the strength of lions and of saints
for whatever bold endeavors they may risk.

He vanishes.

GUESTS

Aaahhh! Aaahhh! Aaahhh!
Bliss! Bliss! Bliss!

General dance.

AFTERWORD: SONG OF SONG

Do you ever hear it?
Do you know
               What your voice is
                              Always singing?

Listen!
          It sings
                    (like everything)
as if no song
               were ever sung before like
                         this

It
  Is the song you have been singing
                              All your life

APPENDIX

REFLECTIONS

James Broughton's Films and the Art of Poetry

APPENDIX

REFLECTIONS:
JAMES BROUGHTON'S FILMS
AND THE ART OF POETRY

The images James Broughton projects upon the screen may be embodiments of "energy," but they are doing precisely the opposite of what we are doing: they are dancing, we are sitting.

The promise of film is that it will show us things that we have never seen before or that we may fervently wish to see. Films can fulfill that promise, but they are rather like those fairy tales in which the hero gets his wish but also gets a condition, which renders the fulfillment of the wish null and void. Like memory, films give us access to things we cannot "have," cannot "touch"—things that are highly problematical from a physical point of view.

And for Broughton the ability to touch is the central ability our bodies possess. "The one great fear in the west," he writes, "is that of touch":

> It is considered slightly indecent to be physically
>   demonstrative. And yet this
> is the way that the body can be initiated into the wonders
> of   bodily experience,
> to feel in the realm of deep feeling the embraces of the
>   gods... This is not an
> exercise in longing nor merely a sexual maneuver. This is
>   the physical Way to
>   the Spirit.

We certainly can't touch the people or objects in a film or in a poem. Aren't movies and poetry precisely the opposite of what Broughton advocates? Aren't they, precisely, "an exercise in longing," pure embodiments of frustration?

Yes, but Broughton has a way of joining polar opposites. How many films have presented us with magical areas—Oz's, *Cabinets of Dr. Caligari*—"places" in which one "watches things," areas in which anything can happen? These areas are deliberate analogues of the movie theater. This technique of imaging the movie theater within the film is a way of drawing us more deeply into the film's action as we perceive (sometimes only at a subliminal level) physical parallels between our condition and that of the film's characters—and as our inability to "touch" becomes our ability to "feel."

Broughton's playground is an obvious analogue to the playhouse, both in his play, *The Playground* and in *Mother's Day*. The Marin County woods in *Dreamwood*, the "pleasure garden" in the film of that title, the valley in *The Bed* (even the bed itself), the house with the photograph album in *Mother's Day* are all versions of the "place" in which the audience is situated. Directors as different from Broughton as Alfred Hitchcock, Stephen Spielberg and Bernardo Bertolucci have all employed this technique.

Nevertheless, there is a considerable difference between representing the movie theater as a house with a photograph album, as in *Mother's Day*, and representing it, as Bertolucci does in *The Last Emperor,* as the Forbidden City of China. The park, the valley, the bed, even the photograph album are extremely familiar, easily accessible "places." They are exactly the opposite of Bertolucci's *Forbidden City.* Similarly, though there is a good deal of sex in some of Broughton's films, the point of the sex is hardly that we can't (or shouldn't) "have" it, which is the point of the sex in films like *Fatal Attraction* or almost any Hitchcock production. Broughton focuses on "our bodies"—to use the phrase he repeats in *The Golden Positions*—precisely because we do have access to them. He is not trying to emphasize the exoticism of his material. Even the (in every sense of the word) marvelous parade through town in *Testament* is, after all, a common enough occurrence—a parade through town—and we are aware throughout the film that Broughton is as much a good, native son of Modesto as he is an exotic stranger.

Bertolucci, caught at once in the competitiveness of the commercial cinema and in the imperatives of the mass market, is showing us "places" that we will very likely never get to see—which is like letting us look at objects that we will never be able to buy. Broughton isn't trying to "sell" us anything. He is trying to show us the magic inherent in what we already have, trying to awaken us to a sense of our own potentialities, to what "our bodies" can do for us.

Though neither Broughton nor anyone else can annihilate the distance between the spectator and the events on the screen—a distance in which, be it said in passing, "our bodies" are situated very problematically indeed—his use of film, unlike Hitchcock's or Bertolucci's, has been consistently to diminish that distance, to insist, as Walt Whitman put it, that "what I assume you shall assume, / For every atom belonging to me as good belongs to you." From *Erogeny*:

       Reach
              Touch
                     Discover

       We are hemispheres
              ebbing and flowing
       We are continents
              meeting

       Discover
              My oases
                     Explore me...
       Cherish
              Touch
                     Connect

Broughton's works are thus demonstrations of the physical bases of the arts, of the grounding of art in "our bodies," and this applies not only to his films but to his poetry.

When Shelley began his great poem, *Epipsychidion* with "My Song, I fear that thou wilt find but few / Who fitly shall conceive thy reasoning," or when Yeats began his *Collected Poems* with "The Son of the Happy Shepherd," neither poet expected the reader to take the word "song" too literally. (In fact, both poets expected the reader to recognize that they were alluding to certain books—in Yeats's case, Blake's "Songs" of Innocence and Experience and in Shelley's, Dante's *Convito*.) In their works the word "song" was for the most part a literary convention. The primary way of disseminating poetry for these poets was not—as it was for Homer—the mouth, the sound of the poet's voice, but the page. And the page is taken in, not with the ears, as a "song" is, but with the eyes.

Still, neither Shelley nor Yeats takes very much advantage of that fact: neither of them uses the page to any significant extent, nor even to the extent that Broughton uses the page in the poem I have just quoted. For them, the white space of the page is essentially neutral. This was not, however, the case for Stephane Mallarme when, in 1897, he published *Un coup de des jamais n'abolira le hazard* (*A Throw of the Dice Will Never Abolish Chance*), a poem in which the silence and whiteness of the page is anything but neutral.

Un comp de des marks the very first moment in which a modern poet admits that he is working with a page and that the page itself, even the entire book, can be used for expressive purposes. One of the terms Mallarme uses to designate the page is toile, which means, among other things, "sail"—like the page, white—and "canvas," what a painter uses for his art. Beginning with that poem, modern poetry embarks upon an enormously important experiment, an experiment, which continues into the present day. It is an experiment with specifically visual experience. Mallarme not only accepts the silence and whiteness of the page as the primary means for the dissemination of his poetry; he makes active us of it.

This is not the place to enter into the historical ramifications of *Un coup de des*, but suffice it to say that that poem gives birth to an extraordinary series of experiments with typefaces, with white space, with patterns, with letters (as in Apollinaire and E. E. Cummings), with "field" techniques, with all sorts of essentially visual phenomena. In addition, poets begin to claim that their work is grounded in the visual, in "images," and for the first time it is possible to argue—as C. Day Lewis does in *The Poetic Image* (1947)—that "imagery" is the very basis of poetry.

The connection of all this to Broughton is perhaps already clear. Broughton is one of the few significant modern poets to have taken the concern with "imagery" to one of its possible conclusions. The whiteness of the page becomes in his work the whiteness of the screen, which Broughton "fills" with "images" of all sorts. Indeed, he is able to go even further than that. By adding a soundtrack to his films he is able to give poetry back precisely what the page took from it: the sound of the poet's voice.

His films are thus fascinating responses to a problem central to all modern literature. What we call "writing" is traditionally grounded in speech, in the aural, yet it depends for its dissemination not on the aural but on the visual, on the page. Broughton's films raise the question of whether there are not—as indeed there seem to be—alternative ways of presenting "writing."

— Jack Foley

ABOUT THE EDITOR

"Jack Foley is doing great things in articulating the poetic
consciousness of San Francisco."
—Lawrence Ferlinghetti.

Jack Foley is an innovative, widely-published San Francisco poet and
critic and was a longtime friend of James Broughton. Foley is well-
known throughout the Bay Area and elsewhere for his spoken-word
performances—performances which often involve "choruses" (multi-
voiced pieces) presented jointly with his wife Adelle. Foley's work
has been described by *Heaven Bone* magazine as "evolving from the
linguistic musical tradition of the original S.F. 'Beat' poet/performers
and extending that eye, ear, and voice of penetrating clarity into a
modern mythology." Poet Dana Gioia called Foley's poetry "that rare
commodity—genuinely avant-garde poetry ... experimental poetry with
depth and intelligence as well as intensity." James Broughton described
Foley's choral pieces as "androgynous."
    Since 1988, Foley has hosted a show of interviews and poetry
presentations on Berkeley radio station KPFA. "Foley's Books," a review
column, appears regularly in the Gazebo section of online magazine, *The
Alsop Review*. Foley is also a contributing editor of the Berkeley journal,
Poetry Flash. Foley's poetry books, all of which feature accompanying
CDs or cassette tapes, include *Letters/Light—Words for Adelle, Gershwin,
Adrift* (nominated for a BABRA award), *Exiles,* and (with Ivan Argüelles)
New Poetry from California: Dead / Requiem. His *Greatest Hits: 1974-2003*
appeared from Pudding House Press—a by-invitation series.
    Two companion volumes of Foley's essays and interviews appeared
from Pantograph Press: *O Powerful Western Star* and *Foley's Books:
California Rebels, Beats, and Radicals. O Powerful Western Star,* which has
the distinction of being the only book of critical essays to include a CD
on which the author performs some of the work in the book, received
the Artists Embassy Literary/Cultural Award 1998-2000. Foley is also
the editor of *The "Fallen Western Star" Wars,* a compilation of responses
to Dana Gioia's controversial essay, "Fallen Western Star" and the
translator of a selection of songs by the French songwriter, Georges
Brassens. Foley's play, *The Boy, the Girl, and the Piece of Chocolate* was
recently made into a film by Alabama filmmaker Wayne Sides.

tain
go to
they were
that it did
com
clha
was
the

CPSIA information can be obtained
at www.ICGtesting.com
Printed in the USA
FFOW03n1251010416
22893FF

9 781938 246050